ANCIENT AND MODERN

St Canice, Kilkenny (W.H. Bartlett)

Ancient and Modern

A Short History of the Church of Ireland

Robert MacCarthy
Dean of St Patrick's

FOUR COURTS PRESS

Set in 11 on 13 Times New Roman
and published by
FOUR COURTS PRESS LTD
Fumbally Court, Fumbally Lane, Dublin 8
e-mail: info@four-courts-press.ie
and in North America by
FOUR COURTS PRESS
c/o ISBS, 5804 N.E. Hassalo Street, Portland, OR 97213.

First published 1995. Reprinted 2000

A catalogue record for this title
is available from the British Library.

ISBN 1-85182-205-4

Printed in Ireland by
ßetaprint Ltd, Dublin.

CONTENTS

To the memory of the
Right Reverend Robert Wyse Jackson, L. L. D., L I T T. D., D. D.
Bishop of Limerick

PREFACE

This book originated in a series of six lectures which I gave to a lay audience in Kilkenny, at the invitation of the Reverend Hueston Finlay, now Chaplain of Girton College, Cambridge, and then Bishop's Vicar in St Canice's Cathedral.

I have deliberately retained the spoken format, and the local illustrations, which will, I hope, help to commend it to a non-specialist readership. I dedicate it to the memory of Bishop Robert Wyse Jackson, who knew more about the Church of Ireland than anyone else of his generation and from whom I learnt so much.

Although this is in no sense an official history, I am glad to acknowledge a grant in aid of publication from the Church of Ireland.

James Usher, Archbishop of Armagh, 1625–56, an engraving by
G. Vertue after a painting by Peter Lely.

THE EARLY CHURCH AND THE CELTIC CHURCH

Baptism & Eucharist are necessary, ministry is inevitable but its forms are not, all else must be judged on its merits—how far do they assist the expansion of the gospel of Christ, how far do they contribute to the extensions of the Kingdom?

That is the yardstick by which all aspects of Church organisations have to be judged, whether for far-off times or today. We have to cover too rapidly some extraordinary developments in the early years of the Church, the effects of which are still very much with us today. We shall see the Church being taken up—taken over—by the Roman empire and then that Church managing to survive the break-up of Rome, which was not just an Empire among many (as we tend to think of it) but the *only* form of civilisation then known to man, and therefore its break-up seemed the end of the world to most people who were in a position to think at all: of course, the majority of people were simply taken up with where their next meal was coming from.

If we think that doctrinal disputes are the invention of the twentieth century, we will be much mistaken: there were doctrinal disputes right from the beginning, and indeed it is probably true that doctrinal disputes have never, even in the Reformation period, been fiercer than in the first two centuries of the Church's life. The Creeds which we find such a conundrum today are really the carefully balanced treaties by which some of those disputes were settled.

I want to mention just one, because it was the cause of the first-ever involvement of the secular power in the Church's affairs. A certain bishop of Antioch named Paul of Samosata who withstood Origen's doctrine of the pre-existence of the Word was denounced by his fellow bishops to the pagan emperor, Aurelian, in about 272 and Aurelian decided that the legal ownership of Church buildings should be assigned 'to those whom the bishops of Italy and Rome should communicate in writing'. There you have the long shadow of the dominant role of the Church of Rome in the history of the Church.

But before that occurred, the church had had an experience of persecution which one would have thought would have put doctrinal disputes at the bottom of its concerns.

By this time, Christians were widely disseminated in society throughout the empire and were sitting ducks when persecution came under the Emperor Decius in c.250—the bishops of Rome, Antioch and Jerusalem were martyred and many more went into hiding. Under Valerian meetings for worship were forbidden and the bishops and senior clergy were picked out for execution. But the Church survived, as it always does under persecution (as in Russia in our own day), and perhaps the worst legacy was the wave of internal divisions and collaborators—to which persecutions usually give rise. Persecution ceased in c.260, only to be renewed with greatly increased force under the Emperor Diocletian in 304. There were two interesting things about Diocletian: (i) he died at York in 306 (persecution was never severe in Britain, some churches were destroyed, but no one was executed), and (ii) he was succeeded by his son, Constantine. The latter's Christianity seems to have come from a Christian half-sister named Anastasia.

Very many things in all our Churches date back to this 'officialisation' of Christianity under Rome: the word 'diocese' is a Roman secular term; the black scarfs we clergy wear was a mark of authority in the Roman empire and is still worn cross-wise by judges in England for the very same reason.

But no sooner did the Church become Established than it began to tear itself apart once again with doctrinal disputes. The dispute which took up most of the fourth century was called Arianism after the opinions of Arius, a priest of Alexandria, who taught that the Son was not of one substance with the Father and belonged to the created order. This was the unlikely spark that set the whole Christian world ablaze; of course, doctrinal disagreements quickly became entangled with questions of order, discipline and authority and in fact with the gradually emerging divisions between the two parts of the Empire—the Greek Orthodox East and the Roman-dominated West. The whole wretched business dragged on until the final suppression of Arianism by Emperor Theodosius I in 381—which is not all that long before the arrival of Christianity in Ireland, which we are wrongly inclined to date from the arrival of St Patrick in 432.

Irish people in general are inclined to view the Celtic period through a romantic mist, while Church of Ireland people are inclined to see the Celtic Church through a similar haze and to imagine that it was some early form of Protestantism of which we and we only are the spiritual heirs—both assumptions I hope to put to flight. The Celts and Gaels were simply one of successive waves of invaders to have come to these shores: they turned up during the first century BC and they treated the existing population in much the same way as they themselves were to be treated by later invaders, that is they killed some, dispossessed others, and compelled the rest to pay tribute. Their conquest of Ireland was not complete before the fifth century, the same century in which Christianity came to Ireland. 'But long before that the Gaels had imposed their language and their legal system on the whole country and Gaelic historians and genealogists had reconstructed the past so as to obscure the great diversity in origins of the population' (J.C. Beckett).

The first contact of our Celtic forebears with the Christian religion was in the unpromising role of heathen barbarians whose savage raids helped to break down the declining Roman civilisation of Britain. That is the first unpalatable fact—that our Christianity came from Britain. Secondly, there was some Christian presence in Ireland before St Patrick. But scholars are agreed that Patrick was the most successful. His dates are probably wrong, and probably also the well-known story of his minding cattle on Slemish in Co. Antrim. But after Patrick, the Church was firmly established and paganism on the decline, whereas before him Christians in Ireland were few and scattered. It is worth noting too that the introduction of Christianity to Ireland was accomplished peacefully: there are no early Christian martyrs in Ireland, though no doubt later chroniclers would dearly have liked to have some to record and celebrate.

This early Irish Church was like no other Church before, then or since. In particular, it bore no resemblance in its origins to either Roman Catholic or Church of Ireland Churches today—which are almost carbon copies of the monarchical episcopate developed in the middle ages and which some of us would consider to have long outlived its usefulness. Instead 'Bishops were advanced to the Order for pre-eminent holiness and sanctity' (W.H. Rennison). The whole organisation of society in Ireland was different to Roman Britain: the unit of government here was not territorial but an ascending hierarchy of kinship groups, that is, extended families dominated by a ruling family, such as the Kavanaghs and the O'Moores of Leix.

Bishops were awarded to powerful family groups—St Patrick was supposed to have appointed 300—and the religious centres which opened were 'family/tribal monasteries', most of which would have had a bishop 'on the staff' but not at its head. A well known example is Conleth of Kildare. Irish monasteries were quite unlike medieval ones and took the form of a little town of wooded huts with maybe a small stone church in the centre. These monastic towns would have contained hundreds of 'monks'. An abbot was usually elected from among the family of the founder and so you can see how everything was kept 'within the family'. Ossory is simply a tribal kingdom, and the see had its origins in the monastery of Seir Kieran at the end of the fifth century; only with the coming of the Normans was the see moved to their great new centre of Kilkenny, which soon could boast a brand new cathedral to symbolise how things were to be run in future—on a territorial basis.

This curious Celtic organisation is fairly well-known, but very little is known about Celtic spirituality. Here is a summary of such knowledge as we do have, provided by John Macquarrie, one of the best-known English theologians of the present day:

> Although it (Celtic spirituality) belongs to a culture that has almost vanished, it fulfils in many respects the conditions to which a contemporary spirituality would have to conform. At the very centre of this type of spirituality was an intense sense of presence. The Celt was very much a God-intoxicated man whose life was embraced on all sides by the divine Being. But this presence was always mediated through some finite this-worldly reality, so that it would be difficult to imagine a spirituality more down-to-earth than this one.
>
> The sense of God's immanence in his creation was so strong in Celtic spirituality as to amount sometimes almost to a pantheism . . . But perusal of typical Celtic poems and prayers makes it clear that God's presence was even more keenly felt in the daily round of human tasks and at the important junctures of life. Getting up, kindling the fire, going to work, going to bed, as well as birth, marriage, settling in a new house, death, were occasions for recognising the presence of God . . . The model for understanding God was the 'High King',

> but among the Celts the High King was never a remote figure
> . . . the king was always among his people as well as over
> them. When God is conceived on such a model, he cannot
> become too distant and likewise his creation cannot become
> so profane and godless as to arouse the acquisitive and ag-
> gressive spirit of irresponsible concupiscence.[1]

These themes can be most easily examined in some of the hymns
from ancient Irish sources which are to be found in our Irish Church
Hymnal and alas are not used nearly enough—apart from the over-
used 'Be Thou My Vision . . .'. What Macquarrie calls 'immanence
in his creation' can be best illustrated by a perusal of St Patrick's
Breastplate—the theology of which I find very attractive. Certainly
in all our Churches today we have lost any theology of God being
served and encountered in our daily tasks. Irish Roman Catholicism, which affects us all without our knowing it, has in recent
centuries been fiercely dualistic in emphasis.

It is now time to turn from the least known to the best known
feature of Irish monasticism—its devotion to the bible and in particular the astonishing decorative skills which it lavished on the actual
text of the New Testament. There has been a listing of thirty-seven
works, ten on the Old Testament and twenty-seven on the New Testament, composed in Ireland or under Irish influence between 650
and 800. Of course, all these great manuscripts were written in Latin,
the universal language of educated people throughout Europe for
more than 1000 years (the development of Irish as a written language incidently, was entirely the work of the early monasteries).
Many of the Latin manuscripts produced in Irish monasteries contain words or phrases in Irish in the margins or between the lines—and
an important work in Irish is by a monk called Aengus of Tallaght,
who started off in Clonenagh, and then founded Dysart Enos, both
in Leighlin diocese, before joining forces with St Maelruain in
Tallaght.

The ability to read was virtually confined to ecclesiastics—so
the great truths of the gospel and the contents of the Bible had to be
communicated first verbally, but then visually. In the Celtic Church,
the high crosses seem to have fulfilled this purpose, but they also
served as memorials of important individuals and to mark great oc-

---

1   *In Paths of Spirituality*, quoted in *Irish Spirituality* ed. M. Maher, p. 7

casions in the history of a particular monastic foundation. Fortunately, there are plenty of examples to choose from in every area—for example Ahenny and Killamery on the western border of Ossory; Moone and Castledermot just over the border in Glendalough to the east. In addition to the illuminated manuscripts and the carving of the crosses we also have a great heritage of metalwork from the Celtic Church in the shape of covers for sacred books and shrines for relics of the saints.

It is difficult to ascribe any one reason for this great flowering of Art—the like of which has certainly never been seen since in this country. Here are some of the factors and individual scholars have put varying weight on them:

- Ireland at that time was a haven of peace and stability for the rest of Europe which was witnessing the break-up of the greatest civilisation the world has ever known.
- The Irish monasteries—at least till the coming of the Vikings—were exceptionally stable elements in Irish society due to their close connection with the tribal and family basis of Irish society.
- Irish spirituality was very open to the development of art for art's sake, taking the world of nature as its model: they made no distinction between the sacred and the secular.
- The lack of corporate organisation in Irish monastic life—each monk would have his own separate hut—meant that individuals could 'do their own thing' at their own pace and at their own timetable. The hermit monks on Mount Athos are the only examples today. Artists never flower under regimentation!

The missionary outreach of the early Irish Church is perhaps easier to explain: any living Church will be a missionary one in some sense or other. The ironic fact is that at the same time as Patrick and his successors were establishing Christianity in Ireland, the Anglo-Saxon invaders were destroying it throughout a great part of Britain, from where St Patrick had brought the faith to Ireland. The British Church more or less folded up, and it fell to Irish monks to evangelise the south of Scotland, the north of England and subsequently large parts of the continent of Europe from which Roman civilisation had been obliterated by the barbarian invaders—including much of south Germany, Switzerland and northern Italy.

The greatest figure of this Irish diaspora was undoubtedly Columba—a monk, never a bishop. Whatever about legendary stories, he certainly founded Iona (in 563) which was the powerhouse for the subsequent conversion of northern England through Aidan of Lindisfarne (arrived 635) and Cuthbert of Durham (687). Columbanus set out from Bangor to evangelise the Frankish invaders of Gaul and he eventually got as far as Italy. St Killian is the apostle of what is now Saxony. St Gall has left his name to the canton in Switzerland where he was based. The Irish monks were what we would now call travelling evangelists—always on the move in conditions which would daunt any modern traveller—and so they were given the Latin name *peregrini*. This Irish missionary outreach was at its peak in the seventh century.

It should, of course, be said that travelling by water then was the equivalent of air travel now: it was the best, the quickest and the most widespread communication network of the ancient world. Ireland was exceedingly well placed for international travel in *that* context. But, easy access to the sea worked the other way too—and was the crucial factor in the Viking raids which from around 800 spelt out the doom of this golden age. The first attack was on Lambay Island monastery in 795, and eventually all the great monasteries were sacked since so many of them were conveniently placed on or near rivers, for example, Clonmacnoise, Monasterboice and Lismore. From this period come the round towers, about which so much has been written and speculated.

Eventually the Vikings began (by the early eleventh century) to settle and wrest portions of the country for themselves. The battle of Clontarf in 1014 meant they had to settle for only part of Ireland: Dublin and most of the present large coastal towns were Viking in origin. The Danes became Christians, but the Danish bishoprics of Dublin, Waterford and Limerick were subject to Canterbury. The Norse raids and subsequent invasions spelt the doom of the old Celtic monastic system, and religion and learning went into decline. The isolation of Ireland was no longer an advantage: the Church in Ireland was cut off from the rest of Christendom and missed out on the revival of religion and culture which was a feature of twelfth century Europe, through it must be said that Ireland has some marvellous Romanesque buildings from that period.

It was inevitable, however, that Ireland should rejoin the western Church and give up its distinctive forms of organisation and the beginning of the medieval Church was signalled by the setting up of a territorial diocesan system at the synod of Rathbreasail in 1111, which was attended by no fewer than 50 bishops, 300 priests and more than 3000 laymen. Our ecclesiastical organisation has remained virtually unchanged in the 800 years that have passed since Rathbreasail, although of course, in the Church of Ireland, the twenty-six dioceses decided on at Rathbreasail have been combined into the twelve bishoprics of today; but the bounds remain the same.

Any discussion of early Irish spirituality would be incomplete without reference to the Ceili De movement—a subject which is invariably omitted from the standard school histories. The words mean 'servant of God' and later came to be Anglicised as 'Culdee'. It seems to have begun at Tallaght, whose founder, St Maelruain, was one of the outstanding figures of the movement:

- It was a Reform movement which took root in the Irish Church of the eighth century.
- Our knowledge of it comes from writings of scribes and anchorites who flourished in the eighth and ninth centuries.
- The writings and prayers make no distinction in subject matter between religious, secular matters or nature.
- They were keen on fasting and penance and distrusted learning for its own sake.
- Each member had to have a 'soul-friend' with whom he would discuss his spiritual progress—it was from this practice that private confession took root in the Irish Church and only later spread to Western Christendom as a whole.

In fact, the Culdees outlasted the Celtic Church. They were introduced to Scotland by Columba and survived at Armagh into the middle ages as an ecclesiastical corporation of married laymen and clergy drawn from a particular clan who not only maintained the worship of a great Church like Armagh, but maintained the fabric too.

THE MEDIEVAL CHURCH

I hope to illustrate much of the history of the medieval Church in Ireland from its architecture; because the architecture is still mostly there all around you—albeit in ruins; it seems to me that the obvious way into the history of the time is by trying to understand what went on in those buildings. From the architectural point of view, there was a striking difference between the Celtic Church and the Church in Europe; this was one of the first things to strike the twelfth century visitors to this country.

In 1142 there were few domestic buildings of stone in Ireland and even kings were satisfied with houses of timber and wattle. Henry II had a wattle palace erected in Dublin on his 1171 visit so as not to offend the native rulers. A visiting high ecclesiastic from Europe, Stephen of Lexington, who came on a visitation in 1228, advised that the king of Thomond should not be taken too seriously 'for such kings have neither castles nor halls, nor even timber houses, or saddles for their horses, but huts of wattle, such as birds are accustomed to build when moulting'.

What was true of domestic architecture was true also of ecclesiastical: the Celtic Church maintained a policy of architectural austerity and even the monastic cities of Glendalough, Armagh and Clonmacnois had no great church as the focus of their religious life. The largest church in existence, the tenth century cathedral of Glendalough, was only sixty-two feet long—without aisles, transepts or chancel. Not until well into the twelfth century was Irish architecture affected and influenced by European Romanesque, and as late as that century wooden churches could be found in major monasteries: the pitched roof of Cormac's Chapel and its pitched gables were probably taken from wooden models.

This is the moment to introduce Malachy, abbot of the great monastery founded by St Comgall at Bangor. The first church he built at Bangor was a timber one which he describes as 'beautiful work in the Irish manner' and he got himself into distinctly hot water when he went to replace it with a stone structure on continental lines, that is cruciform and larger: the locals protested: 'We are Irish, not Gauls.'

Buildings were not the only things Malachy was determined to change. He believed that monasticism as practised on the continent could be the means of breathing fresh life into the Irish Church and making the new structures agreed at Rathbreasail really work.

First he turned to the Augustinian canons. These were rapidly introduced to Ireland (by 1148 over 40 communities had been established), and they proved an effective way of reviving defunct Celtic monasteries. They were often placed in urban centres: these were team ministries of priests living a simple rule; they were not monks. But towards the end of his life, Malachy began to realise the potential of the Cistercians as a reforming instrument and he became a close friend of St Bernard, abbot of Clairvaux, the driving force behind the Cistercians. In fact, St Malachy died at Clairvaux in 1148 while on a visit to St Bernard.

What was new about the Cistercians?

- They were highly structured: nothing could have been further from the easy-going ways of the Celtic monasteries, or even the Canons Regular.
- There was a rigid hierarchy within the monasteries.
- It was an international order: the system of visitation of houses by founding abbots meant that the unity of Cistercian life throughout Europe was vigorously controlled, and there was an annual chapter of all Cistercian abbots which the Irish abbots were obliged to attend.
- All this, Malachy calculated, would enable Cistercian communities in Ireland to withstand the family pressure from local interests and families.

His hopes were realised. Cistercians did become a focus for reform, and Mellifont, the principal Irish Cistercian house, hosted one of the sessions of the reforming synod of Kells. The growth of the order in Ireland was nothing short of spectacular even if one only considers the difficulties of communication in the Ireland of the twelfth century. Mellifont was founded in 1142 and was careful to include both French and Irish monks—Irish novices having already been trained at Clairvaux under St Bernard's eye. Despite initial tensions between the French and Irish, recruits flocked to Mellifont and the number of monks completing their novitiate rose at a tremendous rate.

Expansion was so rapid that within four years, five houses were established, including Baltinglass (1148) and Inishlounaght (1148). Then the daughters founded other houses; for example, Jerpoint founded from Baltinglass in 1160–2. By the time of the Norman invasion, there were eleven houses dependant on Mellifont; these included a Scottish house in the Mull of Kintyre which may have been founded by Malachy himself. By 1170, there were fourteen Cistercian communities in Ireland containing perhaps 500 members. Mellifont alone had 100 monks and 300 laybrothers.

Among the factors that accounted for the Cistercians' success were the following:

- A charismatic leader—Malachy.
- A feeling that the Celtic monasteries had run into the sand, that they had become hopelessly secular through hereditary officers etc.
- A wish to be part of the religious renaissance on the Continent. (English domination of Ireland in recent centuries has made us much less European than we were in earlier times when Latin was the language spoken by all educated people.)
- It wasn't just a Church thing: it had the enthusiastic support of the petty kings and tribal rulers. Present at the consecration of the church of Mellifont in 1157 were the high king, Murtagh MacLoughlin; Donough O'Carroll, the original benefactor of the Monastery; and Devorgilla, wife of the king of Meath. By 1170 four of the five provincial kings had become patrons of the order.
- They were the first to give a religious significance to manual labour and in particular to agriculture. They deliberately sought out uncultivated wastes where they could live undisturbed and in the process became the leading farmers of Europe. In Ireland one of the reasons for their rapid spread was that large tracts of the country were unpopulated and uncultivated. As Gerald Cambrensis, the medieval chronicler, remarked 'Give the Cistercians a wilderness or a forest, and in a few years you will have a dignified abbey in the midst of smiling plenty.'

- Their poverty and ascetic ways of life struck a chord in Ireland
and revived memories of the Celtic saints.

That fateful date 1170 has already been mentioned—the year of the
Norman invasion. At this point I must rapidly sketch what that was
about nationally, before returning to examine its impact—and that
of the Cistercians—on the Church. For a start, to call it an invasion
conjures up notions of a coordinated military operation on a large
scale. It was nothing like that: it was simply a piece of private initiative on the part of some restless Norman barons eager to add to their
wealth and possessions away from the control and financial exac-
tions of their king in England. The quarrelsome Irish chiefs and
petty kings were 'ripe for the plucking'. The pretext came when
Dermot McMurrough, king of Leinster, sought help from the marcher
lords of south Wales to support him in a quarrel with the high king,
Rory O'Connor. As part of the deal, he married his daughter Eva to
Strongbow and when Dermot died in 1171 Strongbow seized and
held Leinster including the all important city of Dublin, despite the
opposition of both the high king and the citizens generally. At this
juncture, Henry II decided he had better take a hand: he arrived in
Ireland with a large army, saw to it that Strongbow and company
would hold their lands as his vassals, and received the homage of a
large number of native rulers. Most importantly for our purpose, he
was warmly welcomed by the Church. He summoned a national
synod at Cashel which decreed many reforms and brought Ireland
into line with English liturgy but not under the control of the Church
in England.

I now turn for a moment to the interesting role of St Laurence
O'Toole—whose heart is the only example of a surviving reliquary
in a Protestant church. Although archbishop of a largely non-Irish
city, he had started life as abbot of Glendalough and, as his name
suggests, he held that office through the old Irish custom of keeping
it in the hands of the ruling family. 'From the O'Tooles and the
O'Byrnes, good Lord deliver us,' as a medieval litany put it. He was
the ideal mediator between the new and the old rulers, and it was
through his influence that Henry II and Rory O'Connor, the last
high king, entered into mutual recognition by the treaty of Windsor
in 1175. More than that, he accepted gifts from the Normans for the
rebuilding of Christ Church and he formally welcomed Henry II to
Dublin. Laurence O'Toole was not alone in seeking an accommoda-

tion with the new power in the land: Gelasius, the aged archbishop of Armagh, paid his respects to Henry in Dublin, accompanied by the white cow on whose milk he lived . . . .

Let us now turn from the national stage to what was happening in one particular part of Ireland. We can confidently date the origin of Kilkenny as an urban centre to the decision of the bishop of Ossory to move his see from Aghaboe to Kilkenny in 1202. At that time, the lord of Kilkenny was William Marshall, one of the first generation of Norman rulers; he gave Kilkenny its first charter in 1207 and ordered his seneschal to divide out the plots of the burgesses and generally lay out the town. This town was not English: it was a Norman-French town, and French was long to be the language of its citizens; for example in the Alice Kyteler affair in 1324, Bishop de Ledrede defended his actions in French.

The early religious history of Kilkenny is a cameo of what the Normans felt they could do for the Church and, equally importantly, what the Church could do for the Normans. William, the earl marshal, founded the Augustinian canons in 1217 in what is now St John's; the Franciscans arrived from Waterford in 1231; and the Dominicans were only four years in Oxford when they opened what we know as the Black Abbey in 1225. But it was the building of St Canice's which was the first and most significant achievement of the Anglo-Norman colony, and its siting at Kilkenny was a measure of the strategic value that the colonists perceived in their new city.

A look at the last bishop in Aghaboe and the first to be sited in Kilkenny will shed a lot of light on the new order. The last bishop in Aghaboe was Felix O'Dullany. Irish as his name suggests, he was a Cistercian and the first abbot of Jerpoint, which he presided over for twenty years prior to his consecration in 1178, and he is buried there. All we know about him is that he had the courage to excommunicate Theobald Fitzwalter, the founder of the Ormonde family, for making away with church lands.

Then came a very different successor in 1202—Hugh de Rous, an Anglo-Norman, an Augustinian Canon and second prior of their house in Kells; it was he who granted the site of Kilkenny castle to William Marshall. After him, all the bishops of Ossory were Normans, and were based in Kilkenny—though it is worth noting that St Canice's was built on an existing Celtic religious site, as the round tower attests (they were careful not to touch the tower).

Kilkenny became very much the flagship of the most successful region of the Anglo-Norman colony in the area centred on the three rivers, the Barrow, Nore and Suir. For the first time Ireland became an exporting country, and the bulk of these exports went not through Dublin, but through New Ross and Waterford, whose combined trade far exceeded Dublin and Drogheda, the ports of the Pale. The chief sources of the region's wealth were sheep and corn. This is where the Cistercians made their economic contribution: they were pioneers in sheep farming and it is no accident that the south-east was peppered with their houses—Jerpoint, Baltinglass, Duiske, Dunbrody and Tintern on the estuary; Kilcooley, Holy Cross, Cashel and Inishlounaght in the west.

But the Anglo-Norman presence in Ireland was soon threatened by the fate which every invader has to face—the threat of absorption into the majority. The Normans sought to prevent this by a series of statues designed to keep them apart from the native Irish. The Irish Parliament itinerated round the chief towns and met in Kilkenny every four years, and so the statues passed by a parliament meeting in Kilkenny in 1366, presided over by Lionel, duke of Clarence, the son of King Edward III, are known as the Statutes of Kilkenny; they aimed at setting a permanent barrier between the two races in Ireland. Intermarriage, the use of the Irish language or dress (riding bare-backed or even Irish hair style!) were forbidden. Of course, like so many laws, they fell largely on deaf ears and when the royal duke had departed, life went on much as before. But what is of concern to our purpose is the way in which the Statutes of Kilkenny re-enacted and strengthened this policy of apartheid in the Church. All bishoprics were to be reserved for the Anglo-Normans and, in the part of Ireland under government control, Irishmen were excluded from all ecclesiastical offices in chapters and religious houses. This segregation was of long standing by 1366 and was fairly consistently maintained: indeed the suggestion is made by J.C. Beckett that in areas where the native clergy were still in control the reforms of the twelfth century had made little impression, bishoprics and religious houses continued to be associated with particular families; this was certainly true of Leighlin diocese in the early medieval period.

Leighlin was, to quote no lesser an authority than Queen Elizabeth I, 'a bishopric seated between the O'Moores and the Kavanagh', and between the two of them the Norman bishops had a job even to retain a toe-hold in their diocese. One of the last of the native Irish bishops, Dermot O'Kelly, built most of the present cathedral and was bishop from 1152 to 1181; his tomb in Leighlin cathedral is still to be seen. Then there is a gap in the succession until the election in 1198 of John, abbot of Monasterevan. I have not been able to discover his nationality but he may have been the first Norman bishop. He died after only three years and an undoubted Norman was elected in the shape of Bishop Herle, who was also a Cistercian monk (of Dunbrody Abbey where he was buried in 1217). He attempted to found a Norman borough at what is now Old Leighlin, and the burgesses were granted the privileges enjoyed by the citizens of Bristol. It seems to have been a complete failure: in 1310 we find Edward II granting revenues to 'built a tower for the defence of the town and to maintain three men-at-arms and two hobblers to protect the inhabitants from the attacks of the native Irish'.

Earlier in 1281, a papal mandate was issued to transfer the see of Leighlin to a 'central, safe and fit place' in the diocese. It was not acted on: bishops of Leighlin continued to have a thin time for the rest of the medieval period and many seem to have been absentees. But John Young, bishop from 1363 to 1384, restored the see house at great expense and was then plundered of all his property by rebels some years before his death. He was present when the Statutes of Kilkenny were passed. Next but one came Bishop John Griffin, who was reported as 'being surrounded and destroyed by the King's enemies and to have no place where he can go or stay or lodge'. By this stage (the end of the fourteenth century), the Anglo-Norman colony was beginning to shrink, and areas such as Leighlin diocese were completely outside the government's control.

I want to turn now to the Cistercian houses and see how they were coping with the policy of apartheid between the two races in Ireland and what was the effect on them. There is no doubt that the readiness of both Normans and native Irish rulers to found and endow Cistercian houses had political as well as religious motivation. It is significant that Donal Mor O'Brien, king of Munster, should found no less than three abbeys on his eastern boundary when he found himself being squeezed by Anglo-Norman settlers; these were Fermoy, Holycross and Kilcooley; they would reinforce his authority, make for prosperity in the region, pray for his soul and maybe provide a refuge in his old age.

the division between Anglo-Norman houses and Irish
came so marked that there were virtually two Cistercian
reland. Between the two groups there was a fundamental
of outlook and of wealth. The Anglo-Normans were usually better endowed and in areas where the soil was rich and fertile:
richest were Dunbrody, Tintern and Graignamanagh, all dependent
on English houses. Soon the contrast was expressed also in architecture. The Anglo-Norman houses, constructed by English-trained
masons, rose from the ground in an austere Early English style and
before long too the difference was expressed in a breakdown of
monastic life in the Irish houses. As early as 1216 what is known as
the Conspiracy of Mellifont took place by which a general visitation
from the headquarters of the Order in France was physically resisted. The gates of Mellifont were shut in the visitors' faces and at
Jerpoint a riot broke out when they appeared.

In 1230 the Anglo-Norman abbot of Fermoy was murdered, re-
putedly by his own monks. What was happening was spelled out
only too clearly by the Abbot of Citeaux: 'There is neither observance of choir service, nor of silence in the cloister nor of the discipline
of the chapter meetings, nor use of the common table in refectory,
nor of monastic quiet in the dormitories according to the manner of
our order.' Monks wandered outside the monastery looking after
their own personal affairs, and some actually lived outside the monastic walls. Monastic lands were not being farmed directly but were
being leased out. Clearly the Irish Cistercians were becoming indis-
tinguishable from the easy-going canons regular of St Augustine
and some of the changes made here in the thirteenth century were
very similar to those which brought all the religious orders into dis-
repute at the end of the medieval period. But the immediate result of
the Conspiracy of Mellifont was that the Irish houses were brought
increasingly in line with English usage; this is demonstrated by the
replacement of Irish decoration and design even at Mellifont, with
the cool perfection of Early English architecture. The middle of the
thirteenth century was a boom period for the Anglo-Irish colony and
the Cistercian houses shared in this property, especially by exploit-
ing the massive demand for wool.

The Black Death in the middle of the fourteenth century put an
end to this period of prosperity and where the Cistercians were concerned it greatly reduced the number of lay brothers, on whom most
of the agricultural activities depended. Thereafter, direct farming

was given up, the land was rented out and there was little to distinguish the abbeys from the other great feudal landlords of the middle ages. Moreover, they got increasingly caught up in the crossfire between the English and Irish which accompanied the weakening of the Anglo-Norman colony; for example, in 1374, Jerpoint complained to the bishop of Ossory that it was so impoverished by war between the Irish and English that it could not fulfil its obligation or offer hospitality. Numbers declined rapidly, and by the sixteenth century only handfuls of monks remained in most of the houses; Jerpoint for example only had seven monks and Kilcooley two, and only in Dublin (eighteen monks) and Mellifont (twenty-one monks) was divine service being sung or the white habit being worn. Long before that, the leadership of Christian life and witness had passed to others, notably the Franciscans, whose vows encouraged them to be on the move among the people as preachers and confessors. One of the most notorious bishops of Ossory was a Franciscan friar—Richard Ledrede, who prosecuted Dame Alice Kytler.

I should, however, refer to a resurgence in ecclesiastical art which seems to have sprung up after the Black Death. The work of illumination of manuscripts was revived and gave rise to the Christchurch Psalter—done in Dublin by an artist from England—and from this time dated the famous east window of St Canice's which the Nuncio, Archbishop Rinucinni, tried to buy in the seventeenth century, only to have it destroyed by Cromwell a few years later. This window was the finest in Ireland, and, according to Bishop Rothe, 'it skilfully depicted the entire life, passion, resurrection and ascension of the Lord, and even that shameless miscreant John Bale and other intrusive bishops after him restrained their violent hands from these windows'. That was how much David Rothe, a man of European education, valued the gift of another European bishop, Richard Ledrede.

But just as the old Celtic Church which had made Ireland known all over Europe as the island of saints and scholars failed at last to meet the spiritual requirements of its people, and needed the changes of the twelfth century to give it new life, so the Church of the Middle Ages became increasingly irrelevant to people's needs: a new beginning was needed.

THE REFORMATION

The roots of the Reformation can really be traced to the invention of printing in the 1450s, for between 1457 and 1500 no fewer than 100 editions of the Bible were published. This had to be contrasted with a growth in popular devotions and popular superstitions which was entirely uncontrolled by the Church—the gap between the religion of the literate and the illiterate grew dangerously wide. The new printing presses were aiding the growth and spread of the new learning with which the figure of Erasmus will always be associated. Erasmus who came from Rotterdam and lived from 1466 to 1536, was not merely one of the greatest thinkers and scholars of his day: he also had the knack of being able to popularise his ideas. He despised ignorance and superstition in the Church, and because he was able to portray the vices and corruption of the Church in a very entertaining way, he could communicate his own contempt to countless other minds.

At the same time as the official Church was losing the battle for the minds of men and women, it was also losing its power of appointment to the European rulers. In 1516, the king of France secured the right of appointment to all the higher posts in the French Church, and by the fifteenth century, the kings of England were already controlling the appointments to bishoprics and even the king of Scotland had obtained the right of appointment to many of the Scottish sees, as did the Emperor Frederick III in Germany. So it was not at all surprising that the secular rulers of Europe should be at the forefront of the Reformation in their territories.

As is well known, the sale of indulgences proved the spark which set alight the German reformation. The particular indulgence at issue was for the building of St Peter's: 'The moment the money tinkles in the collection box, a soul flies out of purgatory' was a popular proverb. Luther, then aged 34, an Augustinian friar and professor of scripture at the University of Wittenberg, was for some time troubled about indulgences. On 31 October 1517, on the door of the

Castle Church, he nailed 95 theses on indulgences and declared that he was ready to defend these at a public disputation. They are conservative in tone and contain none of the central doctrines of the Lutheran Reformation. He was reported to Rome not for an attack on indulgences, but for attacking the authority of the pope.

By 1552 Rome was ready to respond with a papal bull, *Exsurge Domine*, condemning the 41 propositions of Luther as heretical. Luther burnt the bull and was excommunicated. The reason why at this point the whole of Germany didn't go over to the Reformation was because of the German emperor, Charles V, whose power base lay in Naples and Spain; he couldn't sever Germany from Rome without splitting his realm into fragments.

So what did Luther and his followers stand for?

- The power of the Pope abolished.
- The selling of religious rites and offices forbidden.
- A German Bible in every pulpit.
- The liturgy simplified and cleansed of non-scriptural matter.
- Clergy to be allowed to marry.
- Communion in both kinds, but traditional vestments continued to be worn.

The undergirding doctrine was 'justification by faith', that is, the mind and heart came before external expression. But much of Lutheranism is conservative. It reduced the seven sacraments not to two, but to three—Baptism, Eucharist and private confession, which continues to be normal in Lutheran Churches. Luther believed that scripture demanded a belief in the real presence of Christ in the Bread and Wine, but refrained from seeking to define or describe the mystery of the elements. He saw himself not as founding a new Church but as merely trying to purify the Catholic Church from certain abuses.

Two much more Protestant figures were Zwingli and Calvin. Zwingli believed with Luther that the Mass was not a sacrifice, but he differed from him on the question of 'presence'. For him the Lord's Supper was a mere memorial of the Lord's death and a thanksgiving for it; modern Presbyterianism would follow that view today. The more famous Calvin was a generation later than Luther. Calvin's interest was in erecting an authority in the Church to replace the vacuum left by the renunciation of the power of the papacy. His mode of Church government was strictly oligarchic: the pastors chose the pastors, and in Geneva he went far towards setting up a much more theocratic and Church-dominated state than even the popes managed to do. He was also the first Reformation leader to burn an opponent for heresy. From a doctrinal point of view, he taught that there was a special providence of God guiding the particular events of the world and in individual lives: there is no such thing as chance. All this goes by the technical name of 'predestination'.

Let us now catch up with the very non-theological Reformation in England. It began with the dissolution of the monasteries—but even this was gradual. The smaller ones were suppressed in 1536, and the remainder three years later. All was carried through by persuasion, not force. In 1534, the Act of Supremacy was passed, declaring the king to be Supreme Head of the Church of England. But this in a way is to obscure the fact that from 1518 Henry had controlled the Church as well as the State in England. He did this through Cardinal Wolsey who was both his chancellor and papal legate, and he operated with the pope's co-operation. This convenient arrangement came to an end because Henry wished to divorce his wife Catherine, and that put the pope in a predicament. The predicament was not the divorce as such—the pope was well used to obliging European rulers and princes. The reason Clement VII could not oblige was because, since the sacking of Rome in 1527, he was a prisoner of the Emperor Charles V, the nephew of the lady in question.

You probably know the famous story: Thomas Cranmer, appointed archbishop of Canterbury with the pope's approval, granted a divorce on his own authorisation, and the ill-fated Anne Boleyn was crowned queen in 1533. As regards the royal supremacy of the Church, it is clear that it was generally accepted and in particular that the higher clergy made little difficulty about repudiating the pope. An insight into the reality of church life is given by the comment of the archbishop of York, Edward Lee, that an order to read the declaration against the pope in his diocese would not be widely obeyed, since many of his curates could not read, and he had less than twelve clergy capable of preaching.

But of course nothing else changed under Henry VIII except for the placing of a bible in English in every parish church. It was not until the death of Henry and the accession of the boy king, Edward VI, in 1547 that Cranmer and others were able to reveal and put into practice a modest English version of continental Protestantism. Cranmer's great achievement was the First Prayer Book of 1549, in which he had sought to mould the best of the old Catholic liturgy with the new ideas: the preface which we still have in our Book of Common Prayer gives the flavour well of what he was trying to do.

During the reign of Edward VI (1547–53), a conservative Reformation was carried through in England: a new and simplified liturgy in the vernacular with a Swiss doctrine of the Eucharist, a new statement of doctrine (the 39 Articles), churches stripped of images, stone altars and ceremonies forbidden except those expressly provided for in the Book of Common Prayer. But otherwise the ancient system of church government was continued. But the Book of Common Prayer of 1549 could still be taken to teach the real presence in the Eucharist: 'The Body of Our Lord Jesus Christ which was given for thee, preserve etc.' So in 1552, a familiar addition was made: 'Take and eat this in remembrance . . .'.

There was not much opposition to all of this in the country—nor support, either. People don't like any liturgical changes: Professor Owen Chadwick has remarked that 'England was not yet a Protestant country: it took the reign of Bloody Mary to make it so.'

Meanwhile what was happening in Ireland? The dissolution of the monasteries was, as in England, a gradual process. The final list was not issued until 1539, and of course this could only be enforced in those areas under government control. Monasteries in areas such as Tyrone, Fermanagh and Donegal continued in existence until the next century. There were some official protests about the suppressions of certain houses, for example the nunnery of Grace Dieu, which provided the only school 'for the womenkind of the whole Englishry of this land'. But the only exception made was Christ Church, Dublin, which retained its property, the prior and monks becoming dean and canons. The only other significant event in Henry's reign was provided by Archbishop Browne's public burning of images and relics. Browne, a former Augustinian friar who had been made archbishop of Dublin by Wolsey, was the only definite Protestant among the Irish bishops at this time. The royal supremacy over the Church in Ireland was accepted by the Irish parliament in 1536, and none of the bishops in the House of Lords dissented; but during Henry's reign the only bishops who could be said to favour reformed opinions were Archbishop Browne and Bishop Staples of Meath. The rest continued on as before, having accepted the royal supremacy, except that a growing number of bishops and clergy were availing of the permission to marry.

It does not seem as if any attempt was made to make the Prayer Book of 1549 available in Ireland: there were no printing facilities in Ireland until in 1551 Henry Powell set up the first printing press in Ireland at Winetavern Street in Dublin. The first book to be printed was the Book of Common Prayer, and it was used for the first time in Christ Church cathedral on Easter Day 1551. Archbishop Dowdall of Armagh left the country rather than authorise its use; most of the other bishops also refused, and in fact only five bishops agreed to it (Dublin, Meath, Kildare, Leighlin and Limerick).

This is the moment to introduce perhaps the most controversial figure ever to have held the see of Ossory—John Bale, a former Carmelite friar who had been imprisoned in England several times in King Henry's reign for his extreme Protestant views. He seems to have been personally chosen by the boy king, Edward. He refused to be consecrated in 1553 in aecordance with the old medieval pontifical which was still in use in Ireland, and got his way in insisting on the new ordinal attached to the 1552 book which had yet been extended to Ireland. Needless to say, he went down like a lead balloon in Kilkenny: his clergy refused to use the new Book of Common Prayer, and clearly they were well matched. Bale professed to be surprised that he had given offence, 'for that I had in my preachings willed them to have wives of their own, and to leave the unshamefaced occupying of other mens' wives, daughters and servants'. He even described his archbishop, George Browne, as 'a brockish swine and a very pernicious papist'.

Bale wrote plays which were performed at the Market Cross in Kilkenny: one was called *The Tragedy of God's Promises*. Bale only lasted a few months in Kilkenny; in July 1553, King Edward died and a really pernicious papist succeeded in the person of his half-sister Mary, who was determined to avenge all the wrongs done to her mother and her mother's religion. Mary was proclaimed queen on 20 August amid unmistakeable demonstrations of popular approval, and in the subsequent procession through the city, the traditional mitre and crosier were carried forcibly before Bishop Bale, he having indignantly refused to touch them. Even Bale's own chaplain urged that a Mass should be said for Edward VI and, during his temporary absence during the month of August, the clergy of Kilkenny restored what he rudely describes as 'the whole papism'—

copes, candlesticks, holy water, censers and crosses and went in procession through the city chanting 'Sancta Maria, ora pro nobis'. Clearly Bale's days as bishop of Ossory were numbered. He had to be rescued from his country residence at Holmescourt where he had caused further trouble by insisting that his workmen should make hay on a Church holy day, the Nativity of the Blessed Virgin Mary. He soon fled to Dublin, and thence to Switzerland.

Let's now turn and see what the earl of Ormonde was making of all this, for the earl was king in Kilkenny then, and for many centuries to follow, and the views of the successive earls will be an accurate guide to the attitude of the leading laity to the successive stages of the Reformation.

We begin with Piers, the eighth earl, who in 1536 founded Kilkenny College in what is now St Canice's Library and which until then was the residence of the prebendary of Blackrath. Piers had cultivated the friendship of Thomas Cromwell, the king's chief minister after the fall of Wolsey; we know that he sent him presents such as a horse, marten skins and acqua vitae, and he did well out of it. He or his heir was granted the extensive properties of the dissolved monasteries of Jerpoint, Kells and Kilcooley. The commissioners were his guests at the castle at Christmas 1538. It is clear that the eighth earl was deeply committed to King Henry VIII's religious policy in Ireland, whatever the nature of his own religious beliefs may have been. Archbishop Browne, a very moderate reformer, preached on the royal supremacy in the cathedral on New Year's Day 1539.

His son and heir, James, who succeeded him in 1539 had been brought up at the English Court and was a moderate reformer. The next (tenth) earl, Thomas, known as 'Black Tom', was, despite a romantic attachment between him and Queen Elizabeth I and his upbringing as a boy at Edward VI's Protestant court, always ambivalent in his religious attitudes. His chief concern in Kilkenny was to keep his relations and clients faithful to him, and he would not put too much pressure on their consciences. He also made sure that all cathedral appointments went to his kith and kin.

It is now time to catch up with what was happening on the wider stage under Queen Mary. She was determined to reverse all the changes of her brother's reign, but not her Father's royal supremacy. She was shrewd enough to realise that she wouldn't get away with recovering the church property taken over by the nobility and gentry. So she made a start by depriving all the married clergy, and that got rid of Archbishop Browne, and the bishops of Meath, Kildare, Leighlin and Limerick—but no charge of heresy was brought against them. As is well known, there was in the second half of her reign in England a systematic persecution of Protestants because of their beliefs. This did not occur in Ireland. Mary reigned for only five years, being succeeded in 1556 by her half-sister Elizabeth, a convinced Reformer, but one determined to tread delicately and mould her policies to the general wishes of her people. She would have no inquisition into the private religious opinions of her subjects—so long as they toed the line in public. When later in her reign she had to withdraw this liberty of conscience, it was for political not religious reasons. An Act of Religious Uniformity was passed in the Irish Parliament in 1560, and the Act of Supremacy re-enacted in the same year. What was the attitude of the twenty bishops summoned to this parliament? This is a controversial question. Bishop O'Fihily of Leighlin had expressed his willingness to conform even before the act was passed. Only two (Meath and Kildare) definitely refused, and were deprived. We know that Tuam and Clonfert definitely took the oath. The rest probably shillyshallied as only bishops can! But it is hard to believe that bishops such as O'Thonery of Ossory would have been subsequently employed on royal commissions if they hadn't conformed. Then in 1566, a set of Twelve Articles were ordered to be subscribed to by all the Irish Clergy, and most seem to have done so. There was no cleavage between the races as yet: the majority who conformed had Irish names.

Well, so much for the clergy; what about the laity? Remember that the area under English government control was steadily shrinking throughout this period. The areas outside government control would not have gone further than what was required under Henry VIII. There was no papal influence but everything else was unchanged. For the most part the ordinary laity followed their chieftain or their lord in matters of religion. But in the coastal towns there is definite evidence that large numbers conformed to the established Church. One one particular Sunday there were 400 communicants in St Patrick's Cathedral, Dublin and 200 at Drogheda.

In Kilkenny one can safely say that not much Reformation zeal was displayed by John O'Thonery, who had been made Bishop in Mary's time and was principally engaged in diminishing the revenues of the bishopric by means of favoured leases to his relations.

Perhaps appropriately, he died in 1565, 'it is said of grief at the loss of some money'. A much more distinguished figure was Peter White, who held the prebendal stall of Mayne. He was one of a Waterford family, and had been a Fellow of Oriel College, Oxford, before his appointment in 1555 as master of the earl of Ormonde's grammar school in Kilkenny. In 1565, he became dean of Waterford, until deprived in 1570 for joining the Church of Rome. Among his pupils at Kilkenny College were two distinguished scholars—Peter Lombard and Richard Stonyhurst—who were prominent historians of the Counter-Reformation.

It was not until after 1570 that the people of Kilkenny had really convinced Protestant clergy (excluding Bale!), nor was a strong episcopal leadership available until Nicholas Walsh was appointed. He was the first bishop to be the son of a clergyman (at least publicly), his father Patrick Walsh being a former Franciscan friar who had become bishop of Waterford. He found Kilkenny and his diocese in a lamentable condition. This is how he described it in a report to the Irish Privy Council:

> that not only the chiefest men of that town (as for the most part they are bent to popery) refused obstinately to come to church and that they could by no means be brought to hear the divine service there with their wives and families (as they are by her majesty's injunctions bound to do) but that almost all the churches, chapels, chancels within that his diocese were utterly ruined and decayed and that neither the parishioners nor others that are bound to repair them and set them up could by any means be won or induced to do so.

But he has a permanent place in Irish history for better and happier reasons. He and a canon of St Patrick's, called John Kearney, produced the first Irish types for printing and got the Book of Common Prayer printed in Irish. He also began a translation of the New Testament into Irish but did not live to see it completed (this was done by Archbishop O'Donnell of Tuam, a native of Kilkenny); it was eventually published in 1603.

The first separate Roman Catholic bishop was not appointed until 1582, but he only resided in Kilkenny in 1583–4, after which he returned to the continent. No doubt Bishop Walsh enforced a degree of outward conformity but the hearts of those who attended the Reformed Services were clearly elsewhere. It was the sort of city where an 'arrant papistical fellow' could be a prebendary of the cathedral for twenty years (W.G. Neely).

Bishop David Rothe was later to claim that the earl of Ormonde was a convert to Rome, but what is without question is that Thomas, tenth earl of Ormonde, was buried in St Canice's with great ceremony according to the rites of the Church of Ireland in 1614. Even though the city was unwavering in its loyalty to the queen, the privy council was informed in 1600 that no cities had masses more openly than Kilkenny and Clonmel, both Ormonde towns.

Archbishop Adam Loftus (Armagh 1563–7; Dublin 1567–1605) saw clearly that Ireland could never be made Protestant simply by bringing it under English rule: something more was needed than political power or even secular education (he founded Trinity College Dublin) and that was the clear teaching of the gospel of Christ. Unfortunately, too few of the clergy of the Church of Ireland were of the calibre of Nicholas Walsh or Adam Loftus—and too many were content to draw the revenues of the Church without any thought or concern for the spiritual duties of their offices.

THE SEVENTEENTH AND
EIGHTEENTH CENTURIES

In an episcopal Church the health of the whole body is for better or worse closely connected with the calibre of the episcopate. Probably never before or since has the calibre varied so widely as at the beginning of the seventeenth century.

We start at the extreme bottom of the scale with the character whom the lord deputy, Thomas Wentworth, described bluntly as 'that wicked bishop', Miler Magrath. A former Franciscan friar, he arrived from Rome in 1566 as the papally-provided bishop of Down and Connor. Within a year, he had made his peace with the government and taken the oath of supremacy. In 1571, he became archbishop of Cashel, a see which he systematically pillaged in favour of his Roman Catholic family throughout the fifty years of his tenure. When a government commission of enquiry was set on foot he immediately entered into negotiations with Rome with a view to returning to his previous allegiance. This served its no doubt intended purpose: the government took fright and cancelled its enquiry. As the lord deputy of the time, Sir Arthur Chichester, wrote:

> The Archbishop is stout and wilful; it were better not to discontent that heady archbishop and leave him at liberty for he is a powerful man among the Irish of Ulster and able to do much hurt by underhand practices, in which he is well experienced.

He died in 1622, aged almost 100, leaving his dioceses in a disgraceful state. He took the precaution of erecting his own monument before his death; it can still be seen in the choir of the ruined cathedral on the Rock. But, alas, Miler Magrath was not alone in making off with the Church's property: many of the leading laity were as bad:for example almost all the rectorial tithes of parishes in west Waterford were owned by the earl of Cork.

At the other end of the episcopal scale was the towering figure of the primate, James Ussher, a scholar of European reputation, whose interests ranged from early Christian antiquities to biblical chronology. He saved the Book of Kells, and it fell to him to minister to Wentworth in the Tower of London before his execution. So great was his reputation that he was left unmolested by Cromwell. Dr Johnson was later to describe him as 'the great Luminary of the Irish Church, and a greater no Church could boast of, at least in modern times'. Almost equally distinguished was John Bramhall, bishop of Derry and then primate at the restoration of Charles II. He and Wentworth, whose chaplain he had been, made a powerful combination to strengthen the position of the Church not just with Roman Catholics but more so perhaps against the rising non-conformists (Presbyterians) who had been introduced into Ireland with the plantation of Ulster. Both were firm supporters of that High Church movement associated with the name of Archbishop Laud in the Church of England. Wentworth, though wise and tolerant towards Roman Catholics, was nonetheless determined to restore alienated property to the Church—regardless of who was holding it—and the dislike which this caused among the Irish nobility was one of the things which brought him to the scaffold. There was the famous case of the earl of Cork's tomb in St Patrick's: Richard Boyle came to Ireland in the late sixteenth century with £27. 3*s*. 2*d*. in his pocket and two flashy suits of taffeta, a rapier and a dagger, and by this stage was receiving £1200 a year from the Collegiate Church of Youghal and £1000 p.a. from parishes in the diocese of Lismore, all for outpayments totalling £106. 13*s*. 4*d*. Wentworth forced him to disgorge the lot obtained through forged deeds and improper leases.

Among other bishops of note was Thomas Ram, bishop of Ferns and Leighlin, who had some success in winning over Roman Catholics to the Church by reasoned discussion and friendly argument based on the scriptures. He bequeathed both an episcopal residence and a library to Ferns and over the door of the house he had this inscribed: 'This House Ram built for his succeeding Brothers, so sheep bear wool, not for themselves but for others.' Alas, the Library was burnt in the 1641 Rebellion. Then there were two remarkable archbishops of Tuam—Nehemiah Donnellan (1595–1609) and William O'Donnell (1609–28), both of whom were Irish scholars and were involved in the production of the first Irish New Testament. Henry Ridley, an Oxford graduate, who had been a schoolmaster in Kilkenny, was bishop of Killaloe (1613–32), succeeding a 'marvellously careless' O'Brien. When he arrived, there were only seven clergy, and by 1622, he had forty-seven (twenty-four of them preachers). He completely re-roofed Killaloe Cathedral.

As already mentioned, Roman Catholicism was strong in Kilkenny and Mass was openly celebrated. A concerted effort seems to have been made to strengthen the established Church by importing a succession of bishops, deans, and canons from England. Oxford graduates were appointed bishops of Ossory in 1610 and 1613 respectively; the latter, Jonas Wheeler, seems to have made some considerable efforts to grapple with the situation: there were just fourteen 'preaching ministers' in the whole diocese of Ossory and six 'reading ministers' and about the same number of churches, but a visitation in 1622 revealed that by now St Canice's had a daily choral service together with a fortnightly Irish service. He also managed to get back some of the see lands illegally leased away by Bishop O'Thonery. There was no retiring age in those days: he died at Dunmore in 1640 aged ninety-seven.

For a view on the leading laity in the seventeenth century, we can do no better than turn to the twelfth earl of Ormonde, who became the first duke of Ormonde and served on three occasions as lord lieutenant. He had been brought up in the household of George Abbot, archbishop of Canterbury, and was as well grounded in Anglicanism as any of those schooled by the Jesuits. Here is his own remarkable self-assessment:

> My father and mother lived and died papists, and bred their children so, and only I, by God's merciful providence, was educated in the true protestant religion, from which I never swerved towards either extreme, not when it was most dangerous to profess it, and most advantageous to quit it.

Yet he maintained close ties with his Roman Catholic kinsmen and tenants and ensured that there was in practice a complete freedom of worship for Roman Catholics throughout his territories. All this stood the Ormondes in good stead when the Protestant community was engulfed by the 1641 Rebellion: 'England's difficulty is Ireland's opportunity.'

But before I turn to that, mention must be made of the celebrated Bishop William Bedell. An Englishman, he came to Ireland in 1627 to be provost of Trinity College Dublin, where he reintroduced the study of Irish and used Irish in the college chapel and he himself undertook to learn the language. After only two years, he was appointed bishop of Kilmore where his memory is still cherished, and indeed the present cathedral was built in the nineteenth century as the 'Bedell Memorial Church'. He did all the things which, if done in every diocese, would have gone far to commend the Church of Ireland to the majority of Irish people. He would only appoint Irish speakers to parishes. He compiled an Irish Grammar and held Irish services himself in Kilmore cathedral on Sunday afternoons, and he published a popular Book of Devotion in Irish, containing the Creed, Lord's Prayer and other prayers and selected passages of scripture. But his greatest literary achievement was the translation of the Old Testament into Irish: he gathered a group of translators round him in his own house in Kilmore and it was finished in 1640. The story of his end is well known: he was imprisoned on an island in Lough Oughter and he died from the effects in February 1642. At his funeral, a Roman Catholic priest called Farrelly was heard to say, 'May my soul be with Bedells.'

In order to see the 1641 Rebellion in context, we need to realise that the English presence in Ireland had been steadily increasing since the latter part of Elizabeth's reign: she had begun the idea of plantations of loyal subjects of the crown from England in tracts of country confiscated from the rebellious Irish landowners. The first was as a result of the earl of Desmond's rebellion in south-west Ireland. Then came the much more extensive and thorough plantations of Ulster during the first part of the seventeenth century, in the reign of James I, and this moreover in an area of Ireland which had little or no connection with the government since the Norman Conquest.

Resentment and fear of a total English take-over of the land of Ireland was building up steadily; Wentworth's business-like policy of 'Thorough' did not help, either. The initial outbreak was planned between the O'Mores of Leix and the Maguires of Fermanagh and clearly the outrages had a sectarian character. This was inevitable since loyalty to the crown was increasingly being judged by whether a person was willing to conform to the State Church. It suited the government to exaggerate the brutality which occurred, but there is no doubt that groups of Protestants, including a number of clergy, were massacred in cold blood throughout the country, but especially in the north-west, and a large number of churches and glebes were destroyed. It added insult to injury when a meeting of Roman Catholic bishops in Kilkenny pronounced the insurrection just and lawful: Bibles and Prayer Books were to be seen used as wrapping paper in Kilkenny's shops and all the churches of the city were taken over for Roman Catholic worship and Bishop Rothe took up residence in the deanery. Bishop Griffith Williams who had only been consecrated in September 1641 and who was also dean, fled to England. The pulpit in St Mary's was smashed to bits and the Communion silver stolen from St Canice's and all its records burnt. All this seems to have occurred just before Christmas 1641, and the Protestants of Kilkenny were fortunate that the countess of Ormonde was in command of Kilkenny Castle, and the equal of any man for courage and determination: here is an eye-witness account of what happened:

> That a little before the 25th December 1641, the city of Kilkenny, being pillaged by the Irish rebels, almost all the pillaged and stripped English came to the castle of Kilkenny as to a place of refuge, some of them naked, others of them hiding their nakedness with thumbropes of straw or hay, some with old rags which the Irish in derision had thrown to them, in which condition they were, by her ladyship, received into the castle, fed and clothed.[2]

The doings of the Confederation of Kilkenny are well-known. Essentially, the participants tried to be loyal to Charles I and get him to grant a legal position to the Roman Catholic Church and yet to repudiate the authority of the English parliament over Ireland. It was a vain hope—and was entertained by Charles I only because of his dire circumstances in England. As in Scotland under Montrose, a part of the Civil War was being played out in Ireland, and Irish Catholics were pawns in what was essentially an English game.

Ormonde was hoping to secure an army of 10,000 men for use by Charles in England. The nuncio, Rinuccini, persuaded Owen Roe O'Neill to refuse to make his troops available and instead turned them on the confederation itself. The game was finally up in August

2   W.G. Neely, *Kilkenny*, p. 86.

1649, when Cromwell landed in Ireland. The Church of Ireland exchanged one persecution for another: the use of the Book of Common Prayer was forbidden, the clergy were all dismissed from their parishes, and Cromwellian preachers installed in their place. By the time of the Restoration, not 100 episcopally ordained clergy were left in the country.[3]

To make a sad story short, the Church of Ireland came into its own again in 'good King Charles' golden days'. In 1661 there was a great service in St Patrick's at which twelve bishops were consecrated, to make up the number of the Irish episcopate. The most distinguished was undoubtedly Jeremy Taylor, who is still the subject of scholarly interest and research. His most celebrated work is a devotional book called *Holy Living*; another is *Holy Dying*, while Bishop McAdoo has recently published a study of his Eucharistic teaching. Unfortunately for Taylor, his episcopate in Down, Connor and Dromore was a torment for him as he was beset by Puritan ministers who had taken over the parishes during the Commonwealth and now refused to conform to the Church of Ireland. At his first coming to the North, he had to declare thirty six parishes vacant.

Elsewhere, the Church quietly got back on its feet until further trouble arrived with James II. Here is how Narcissus Marsh, bishop of Leighlin and Ferns from 1683, described it in his diary:

> I continued quiet in my bishoprick until King James came to the crown, repairing churches, planting curates where wanting, and doing what good I could; but in a little time the Irish Papists grew headstrong and began to be very uneasy to us.[4]

There is no doubt that King James intended to suppress the Church of Ireland and establish the Roman Catholic Church in its place. He made a start with Christ Church cathedral and the chapel of Trinity College, both of which were handed over to Roman Catholic use. Dr William King, who was then in charge of the diocese of Dublin, was imprisoned in Dublin Castle, while the Irish parliament of 1689 disendowed the Church of Ireland.

---

3 See Robinson, Johnston and Jackson, *History of the Church of Ireland*, p. 201.
4 Robinson, Johnston and Jackson, op. cit. pp. 211–12.

In 1690, William of Orange came in on a Protestant wind and a sea-change occurred in Irish land-ownership. Unfortunately, a series of penal laws against Roman Catholics were passed which have ever since, understandably, been seen as a shame and disgrace. Once again the Church of Ireland had to set itself to reconstruction and the story is best told through the life of Archbishop King, who was one of six bishops consecrated on 25 January 1691 in a service reminiscent of the previous great consecration of bishops at the Restoration:

> King's thirty nine years as a bishop were marked by reforming zeal, by great activity in the building of churches and glebe houses, and by the dispensing of extensive and wise charity. He gave £1000 for the founding of 'Archbishop King's Professorship of Divinity', for the improvement of theological instruction in Trinity College. Above all, he was a man with a fervent sense of his calling to be a minister of Christ. It was typical of his character that he should regret his appointment as a Lord Justice on the ground that 'it may obstruct my proper business as a Bishop, which I could never answer.' His religion was sincere and devout, and it was the driving force behind his concentrated years of labour. Perhaps the best epitaph to his memory may be taken from a letter written by himself—'I thank God I am willing to be at any pains, and to venture anything for Christ's sake.[5]

It is well known that the clergy of the Georgian era were at best uninspiring and at worst time-servers, only interested in amassing large incomes. The wealthier bishoprics were used unashamedly to reward the favourites of the government or viceroy: there was an acknowledged ban on Irish born clergy becoming primate, and all the wealthier livings went to the younger sons of the nobility and gentry: a good Kilkenny example is the Hon. and Very Reverend Joseph Bourke, whose father was both earl of Mayo and archbishop of Tuam, and who was dean of St Canice's for no less than forty eight years from 1795. The deanery, prior to disestablishment, had no parochial duties attached to it, and Dean Bourke was also vicar of Offerlane, Co. Laois, from 1797 to 1835.

5   Robinson, Johnston and Jackson, op. cit. pp. 217–18.

But there were nonetheless some very distinguished bishops in the eighteenth century: pride of place must go to George Berkeley, who was educated at Kilkenny College; his metaphysical theories were to mark a new stage in European thought. He was also the first missionary in the post-Reformation Church of Ireland: he resigned the deanery of Derry (worth £1000 p.a.) in 1728, to found a college in Bermuda. The various government grants he had been promised fell through and he got no further than America, where it is said he did more for religion and learning than he could ever have done in that small island. All was not lost: his exploits caught the imagination of Queen Caroline, and she secured his appointment as bishop of Cloyne in 1734.

Almost equally distinguished were two bishops of Ossory, Pocock and O'Beirne. Pocock, who first came to Ireland under the patronage of his uncle, Bishop Milles of Waterford and Lismore, held a number of sinecure posts in that diocese between 1725 and 1756. He was archdeacon of Dublin 1746–56 and bishop of Ossory for ten years from 1756. He was a Fellow of the Royal Society and a very distinguished orientalist whose volumes on Syria are still consulted. But he did more than travel in foreign parts: he was a most conscientious bishop of Ossory, restoring the cathedral and several churches in the diocese. He founded the Pocock school outside Kilkenny. He encouraged the study of Irish history and patronised Mervyn Archdall, the Irish antiquarian.

Then there was Bishop Thomas O'Beirne, who was a convert from Roman Catholicism for whose priesthood he had actually been in training in France. There he fell in with the duke of Portland, who became his friend and patron and the fact that the duke was lord lieutenant of Ireland in 1762/3 was no doubt a factor in his subsequent career. He was rector of Longford at the same time as his brother was the parish priest! He was bishop in Kilkenny for three years from 1795, during which time he revived the office of rural dean, but his main work was done in his twenty-two years in Meath when he succeeded in stamping out absenteeism and in building numerous schools and churches (no less than fifty) and glebe houses.

But these great figures apart, the eighteenth century clergy were a pretty soporific lot and a new movement of the spirit was long overdue. The herald of this was John Wesley, who first set foot in Ireland in 1747 and preached his first sermon in St Mary's, Mary Street, Dublin. Over the next forty two years he was to come to

Ireland again and again and preach through the length and breadth of the land. Wesley's labours laid the foundation for the Evangelical movement, but it is well to emphasize that Wesley never intended to leave the Church of England or to found a new denomination. Indeed one of his rules was as follows: 'Keep to the Church. They that do this best, prosper most in their souls. I suffer no meetings under any pretext to be held during Church hours. When Methodists leave the Church, God will leave them.'

But let the last word on the eighteenth century be an encouraging one. On Christmas Day 1801, there were no fewer than 430 communicants in St Mary's Church, Kilkenny.

THE NINETEENTH CENTURY

I have said that the Georgian Church was sadly in need of a new movement of the spirit and that John Wesley was the herald of it. This chapter will be taken up with charting the course and nature of his new movement—one that transformed both the clergy and the worship of the Church of Ireland and played a major role in ensuring that the Church of Ireland would not merely survive Disestablishment, but take it in its stride and be the better for it.

In this book, I have tried to illustrate the history of the period through local events and local figures where possible, and fortunately we can do this very effectively where the evangelical revival is concerned. John Wesley had been a regular visitor to Kilkenny. His 1767 visit had been billed well in advance as a star attraction and he preached in the Tholsel to a 'prodigious concourse'. But the greatest single force for change in the pattern of Kilkenny religion was the ministry of Peter Roe at St Mary's, 1805–41. There was a consistent concern for conversion and evangelical religion in Roe's ministry that would have been beyond the understanding of the Georgian clergy whose attitudes were well exemplified by Roe's bishop, Robert Fowler. The son of an archbishop of Dublin, he was Dean of St Patrick's at scarcely twenty-six years of age, and his diary which he kept of his exploits on a continental trip suggests that he was without spiritual interests, to put it mildly. He did not omit to appoint his son, the Reverend Luke Fowler, to the rich prebend of Aghour which the son then held for a record spell of sixty-two years. Peter Roe inhabited a different world. The nineteenth-century revival was spear-headed by a whole phalanx of societies: there was a society to enliven almost every aspect of Church life, and the sad remnants of them are with us today.

Roe was responsible for founding the first clerical society in Ireland, the Ossory Clerical Association in 1800. It is hard to imagine nowadays the impact of this: it was the means by which the clergy were themselves evangelised and professionalised and given a sense of common purpose. Previously they saw themselves as independent place-holders with no necessary contact or interest with other clergy or indeed their bishop. Of course, these clerical meetings were denounced as 'hotbeds of dissent', but there is no doubt that in time they transformed the face of ministry in Ireland. Other prominent evangelicals in the Ossory Clerical Association were Robert Shaw of Fiddown and Henry Irwin of Castlecomer. On the wider stage, the Hibernian Bible Society was founded in 1806 and three years later the Sunday School Society for Ireland. In 1810 came the Church of Ireland Jews Society and in 1814 the Hibernian Church Missionary Society (at its first meeting in the Rotunda the collection amounted to nearly £500). Indeed for almost the first time since the days of the early Irish Church, church interest began to be directed outside Ireland in a most remarkable way. The modern missionary movement hardly lasted 150 years and was inevitably associated with the astonishing growth of the British Empire, but it was much more than that as the flourishing Christian presence throughout Africa and India today demonstrates. The Church of Ireland played a remarkable part for its size in that movement. It provided the first Anglican bishop in China; the first archbishop of Ontario; George Lefroy, metropolitan of India and Bishop Pilkington, an early bishop of Uganda. Specifically, Church of Ireland missions were founded at Fuh-Kien in China and at Chota Nagpur in India. Godfrey Day had the distinction of being the only primate to have served as a missionary overseas—in his case at the Cambridge mission to Delhi. The Leprosy mission was founded in Dublin in 1874.

An important force behind the virtual take-over by the Evangelical movement of the nineteenth-century Church of Ireland were the proprietary chapels in the cities. Because known evangelicals could not obtain appointments to the more important parishes, they availed themselves of the powers already available under the eighteenth-century Acts of Parliament, to build themselves churches outside the parochial system. Until the early years of the last century, Dublin was littered with such churches—preaching houses as they were rudely described, for their purpose was to provide platforms for Evangelical standard bearers who were deliberately excluded from parish pulpits.

Thus, the Bethseda Chapel just off Parnell Square became famous through the preaching of B.W. Mathias, who excited the admiration of the great William Wilberforce. Trinity Church, Lower

Gardiner Street (now a labour exchange), was built for John Gregg, later bishop of Cork. St Matthias, Hatch Street was built for Maurice Day, later bishop of Cashel. Other Dublin proprietary chapels outside the parochial system were Baggotrath, Sandford, Zion and Leeson Park. In Belfast there was Christ Church, College Square; in Cork, St John's; in Limerick, Trinity Church. Between them they provided the means by which the new movement could grow, flourish and inevitably in the long run become respectable: a mark of that was, of course, when Evangelicals started becoming bishops. This perhaps is a good moment to survey the episcopal bench.

The first and most astonishing Evangelical bishop was the Hon. Power le Poer Trench, who first became a bishop (of Waterford) in 1802 at an early age simply to pay off his father and brother for voting for the union. He must be the only bishop ever to have been converted as a bishop (this occurred while he was bishop of Elphin between 1810 and 1819) and he went on to become a powerful evangelical leader as archbishop of Tuam between 1819 and 1839. He gave much support to the great wave of conversions mainly in the west of Ireland known as the second Reformation. Then in 1843, Robert Daly was appointed to Cashel. A member of a Co. Galway landowning family, he had been rector of Powerscourt where he had made a notable convert in the person of Lady Powerscourt. As bishop of Cashel, he became a champion of segregated schools in opposition to his metropolitan, Archbishop Whately, who supported the National school system of undenominational schooling, known as the Model Schools. Perhaps the most significant appointment, however, was when John Gregg went straight from a preaching house to be bishop of Cork in 1862, a post in which equally remarkably he was succeeded by his own son. Achilles Daunt went from St Matthias' to be dean of Cork and later incumbents of St Matthias, also to become bishops were Maurice Day, of Clogher, and F.R. Wynne of Killaloe. The first Evangelical archbishop of Dublin was Lord Plunket, whose statue adorns Kildare Place, the original site of the Church of Ireland Training College, which he founded.

Something should be said about the Second Reformation—a movement which can still cause tempers to flare and which is sometimes flung in our faces under the epithet 'souperism'. Two books have been written on the subject by Professor Desmond Bowen. What is not in dispute is that in the first half of the nineteenth century there was a considerable accession of Roman Catholics into the

Church of Ireland, mainly but not exclusively in the west of Ireland. In the diocese of Tuam between 1819 and 1861, seven churches and eleven clergy grew to twenty-seven churches and thirty-five clergy. In Limerick, there were 478 converts in Askeaton alone and several hundred in Doon Here are examples, from Professor Bowen, of how it was done:

> The Rev. John Gregg, the minister of Trinity Church, Dublin, told of how he met a simple, pious countryman at Kilsallaghan on the Dublin-Meath border in 1829 who had found an old Bible without a cover in a trunk. Reading it, the countryman was converted, and when the priest refused to supply him with a whole Bible, for parts of the original were missing, he came to the Protestant rector for help and was led to conform to the Church of Ireland. John Garrett, the Irish-speaking parson of Ballymote, Co. Sligo, attributed many of the conversions he witnessed to the power of the Word when it was preached in the people's tongue:—
> 'I invariably preach in Irish at funerals; and no mandate of the priests can keep the peasantry from crowding around me, and swallowing with mouths, eyes and ears every word I utter, which I impute to my preaching the Gospel without seeming to allude to their errors: and I have several converts who left the mass-house after frequently hearing my Irish sermons at funerals.'

Of course, the charge of proselytism grew sharper when during the time of the famine the Protestant clergy took a lead in helping to keep the people alive. But proselytism was not confined to the west of Ireland by any means, and here is an account of the happenings in Co. Carlow:

> There are indications that during the famine years the priests of the Carlow area lost some of their control of the people, and the Rector of Killeshin, the militant Evangelical Dawson Massy, tried to take advantage of this situation. He welcomed various missionaries to his parish, a 'house of refuge' for converts was established in Carlow town, and a running warfare began between Massy and James Maher, Parish Priest of Carlow. To Massy, Maher was 'an intolerant, fiery, and crafty

persecutor of his fellow-subjects and a rank rebel against his sovereign'. To Maher, Massy represented 'stolid, impenetrable bigotry'. Moreover, the verdict of civilised society was opposed to the church he served, and its weakness was shown by its need for support from the itinerant preachers who had descended on the Carlow area after crossing the channel 'with some new-fangled religion of English manufacture'.

Mention must now be made of two contentious changes which occurred in Church organisation during the 1830s. The first was a prolonged agitation over tithes which did much to damage the standing of the Church of Ireland in many local communities. It eventually flared up into what is known as the Tithe War. The second was the enforced reform of the Church's structures by Act of Parliament: ten bishoprics were suppressed and a number of cathedral posts and their endowments handed over to a body called the Ecclesiastical Commissioners. A similar job was done on the Church of England, and, as far as Ireland was concerned, it was long overdue. Nonetheless, it provoked John Keble's famous Assize sermon at Oxford on National Apostasy: the State had no right to interfere with bishops whose apostolic succession was by divine right.

The pressure for the disestablishment of the Church of Ireland can be dated to the census of 1861 which showed that the Church could claim only one eighth of the population of the whole island. The Royal Commission of 1867 proposed a drastic retrenchment which, if the Church had accepted, it might have survived as an Established Church. There was to be just one archbishop (Armagh) and seven bishops; many cathedral corporations were to be dissolved, and only eight deans were to remain. This scheme was rejected by the Church and, in spite of huge House of Lords resistance, Gladstone put through the Disestablishment Bill which came into effect in 1871. Much hatred of Gladstone by Irish Protestants resulted from this necessary reform. As one would expect from such a devout Churchman as Gladstone, it was a generous settlement: churches and schools in actual use were handed over; glebes could be purchased on favourable terms; and £500,000 in respect of recent private endowments was granted. Everything else was taken by the State. By 1880 over five and a half million pounds of the Church's funds had been distributed to educational purposes, to Maynooth College and the Presbyterian ministry. But what really saved the Church was the willingness of serving clergy to 'compound'—that is, to agree that their stipends for life could be handed over to the Disestablished Body by way of a lump sum on which, of course, the Church could reap the investment income. In addition to this, the State added a further bonus of £300,000 on being freed of the obligation to pay the serving clergy until their deaths.

Disestablishment led to an upsurge of lay initiative in the Church of Ireland which is happily still with us: over the fifty years from 1871 when the Church's population declined by one fifth, annual giving increased six-fold.

The archbishops at the time of Disestablishment were in sharp contrast to each other. The primate was a classic example of the tight grip with the aristocracy had kept on the more lucrative posts in the Church throughout the eighteenth and nineteenth centuries. He was Marcus Gervais Beresford, who in 1862 had succeeded his cousin Lord John George Beresford in the primatial see. Between them the Beresfords had reigned in Armagh for sixty four years of the entire century (Armagh was more lucrative in the old days than the see of Canterbury). Marcus Gervais was without theological or indeed intellectual interests, but his shrewdness and wide connections among the gentry made him an admirable chairman when the new administrative structures came to be set up in the wake of disestablishment. His colleague in Dublin could not have presented a greater contrast. If Armagh had had a succession of noblemen; Dublin had one of English intellectuals. In 1864 the great maverick, Whately, was succeeded by another Englishman, Richard Chenevix Trench, dean of Westminster. He was a High Churchman and one of the greatest thinkers and preachers of the Church of England and the friend of Keble and Pusey. Why he ever agreed to transport himself to a den of unthinking and quarrelsome Low Churchmen is unclear: anyone could have predicted that he would have a miserable time and this he duly did until his death in 1886. He was succeeded by an Evangelical peer in the shape of Lord Plunket, which was exactly the combination which Dublin Protestants would warm to.

Attention should be drawn to that extraordinary vitality and confidence which characterised the Victorian Age as a whole and which is represented in the Church of Ireland by the great burst of church and cathedral building which characterised the mid-Victorian period. The finest thing the Church of Ireland did in the nineteenth century was to build St Fin Barre's cathedral, in Cork. Tuam (by Sir Thomas Deane) and Kilmore (by Slater) were examples of fine but unnecessary buildings in remote situations, while the virtual re-building of Kildare in 1896 and Christ Church in 1878 were both conceived as ripostes to disestablishment.

THE TWENTIETH CENTURY

The immediate aftermath of disestablishment saw the completion of Christ Church, Kildare and Cork cathedrals, but it also saw the new lay-dominated structures flexing their strongly Evangelical muscles in an attempt to revise the Book of Common Prayer in a distinctly Protestant direction. The distress of that tractarian saint, Archbishop Trench, has been described, and it was during his archiepiscopate that another tractarian church in Dublin, St Bartholomew's, was erected to join All Saints Grangegorman, whose tradition dated from 1843—and, of course, their mere existence constituted a red rag to the various Protestant bulls in the General Synod. The Prayer Book debates were full of sound and fury, and centred in particular on the form of Absolution in the order for the visitation of the sick which seemed to suggest that the priest by virtue of his priestly authority had the power to forgive sins. Eventually an acceptable compromise was obtained by substituting the form of Absolution already in use in the Communion office. A row about the Athanasian Creed was neatly resolved by omitting the rubric ordering its use, while some useful new services were added: The consecration of a church and an order for harvest thanksgiving. From this 1879 revision dates the notorious canon 36 forbidding the placing of a cross on the altar—and this was obviously aimed at the three Tractarian churches in Dublin. A more encouraging post-disestablishment development was the foundation of the Church of Ireland Training College in Kildare Place in 1884.

The turn of the twentieth century was marked by two important developments which adversely affected the Church of Ireland: the expropriation of the landlords under the Wyndham and other land acts and the passing of the papal *Ne Temere* decree of 1908, which was to decimate so many rural parishes. The effect of the land acts on church finances was in part mitigated by the launching of the Auxiliary Fund in 1909 which raised a quarter of a million pounds for clergy stipends. The loss of so many Church of Ireland men in the First War or their departure from Ireland as a result of the War of Independence hastened the population decline, while a sharp reduction in the number of rural incumbencies resulted from the passing of the Minimum Stipend Act of 1920 which fixed £400 for incumbents and £200 for curates.

Throughout the first half of the twentieth century, almost all the leaders of the Church of Ireland were staunchly loyalist, not to say Unionist, and they watched with horror what they would have described as 'the rise of Sinn Fein' an attitude in which they would have been supported by 99 per cent of the laity. Moreover, to their shame, the Northern bishops had subscribed to what is known as the Solemn League and Covenant against the acceptance of Home Rule, which was nothing more than a declaration by Northern protestants that they would defy the authority of the crown by force if necessary. It fell to John Gregg as archbishop of Dublin to make some accommodation with the new state in the south, and it was he who solved de Valera's problem as to how the various Churches should be referred to in the 1937 Constitution. But Gregg, and most of those for whom he spoke, remained loyal to the crown and much prized the tenuous links which enabled them to include the king's name in the liturgy until the final declaration of the Republic in 1949.

The Church conferences in the first half of this century did much to illuminate and let fresh wind from abroad into the cobwebbed corners of Irish Church life. Both the first (and it so happened the last) Church Conference took place in Limerick. At that first conference in 1902, visitors from outside Ireland included the bishops of Glasgow and Ballarat, and the dean of Hereford. Perhaps the largest was held in Dublin in 1932 when the Church of Ireland was vigorously celebrating the 1500th anniversary of the coming of St Patrick, in opposition to the Roman Catholics' Eucharistic Congress.

In 1920, women were admitted to select vestries. This innovation Gregg, perhaps surprisingly, supported. Bernard, his predecessor as archbishop of Dublin, not at all surprisingly, opposed. He argued that the sexes were discriminated by nature, yet went on to say that he would like to see the great lady of the parish on the select vestry, but not the gardener's wife. 'Parochial squabbles would be trebled if they admitted women.' This whole movement for women's suffrage had been led by Bishop O'Hara of Cashel, the first dean of the great new cathedral of St Anne which was steadily rising in Belfast. He could hardly have foreseen that women would finally be admitted to the priesthood in 1990, only seventy years after their arrival on the bottom rung of the ladder.

Something should be said about the Church of Ireland's contribution to the ecumenical movement. Where Anglicanism is concerned, this can be dated to the 1920 Lambeth Conference, and its famous appeal 'To all Christian people'. It stated its conviction that the visible unity of the Church will be found to involve the whole-hearted acceptance of (i) the Holy Scriptures as being the rule and ultimate standard of the faith and the Nicene Creed as the sufficient statement of the Christian Faith, (ii) the divinely instituted sacraments of baptism and Holy Communion, (iii) a ministry acknowledged by every part of the Church as possessing not only the commission of Christ, but also the authority of the Whole Body. This would have obtained wide agreement, but alas the Lambeth fathers added what they described as 'the reasonable claim that the episcopate is the one means of providing such a ministry'.

In 1931 talks were initiated with the Presbyterian Church of Ireland which reached some remarkable conclusions, namely 'that each Church fully and freely recognises as a basis for further progress towards union the validity, efficacy and spiritual reality of both ordination and sacraments as administered in the other Church'. This was passed by twenty-four votes to three, but alas among the three was the formidable figure of Archbishop Gregg, who requested that his dissent be recorded. Needless to say, Gregg saw to it that the Report was put into cold storage by the General Synod. Much bitterness was felt in Presbyterian circles that this decision of the General Synod was taken against the advice of the great majority of its own representatives on the negotiating body and talks between Presbyterians and Church of Ireland did not re-open until 1964, when a very different climate prevailed.

This is perhaps a good point to say something about Gregg's influence on the Church of Ireland in this period. Gregg was a curious mixture. Dean Seaver's excellent biography shows that he held markedly liberal views in theology and biblical scholarship, but in all questions about the Church and its ministry he was uncompromisingly conservative. He openly referred to non-episcopalian Christians as 'the deprived children of Christendom'. Thus, while he championed the work of the Anglican and Eastern Churches As-

sociation, he actually boasted that he had never appeared on a public platform in Ireland with a non-conformist minister. The formation
of the Church of South India in 1948 caused ripples in the Church
of Ireland because of the Irish missionary presence in India, and two
Irishmen, one Presbyterian and one Anglican, were serving in India
at the time in the persons of Donald Kennedy and Anthony Hanson.
For primate Gregg, it must have represented the first loophole in
Anglicanism, but there was little he could do about it.

The ecumenical scene was transformed by the visits of Archbishops Fisher and Ramsay to Popes John XXIII and Paul VI and
by the Second Vatican Council, which was warmly welcomed by
the Irish religous orders and more cautiously by the bishops. For
once the Church of Ireland had the right man in the right place in the
person of George Simms, archbishop of Dublin throughout the
1960s—for he was uniquely qualified to lead the Church of Ireland
out of the ghetto which Gregg had so carefully constructed. He was
an Irish speaker and an Irish scholar whose right to make a contribution to Irish Christianity could not seriously be questioned. The
willingness of the Church of Ireland to open its churches and assem-
blies to Roman Catholic participation met an unmistakeable welcome
on the part of the vast majority of the Roman Catholic laity who had
always enjoyed good relations with their Protestant neighbours and
respected their church albeit at a respectful distance. Under George
Simms' leadership, a quite different atmosphere soon pervaded Irish
public life: indeed very quickly the situation became what we are
now well used to—that no 'happening' in any local community is
complete without the presence and participation of the local rector.

On a more ecclesiastical level, ecumenism has been less dra-
matic and many of the Irish Roman Catholic bishops were slow to
implement the new attitudes of Vatican II. Nonetheless the acceptance in practice of our ministry in Ireland by the vast majority of
Roman Catholic priests is now an accomplished fact—and the rapid
pace of practical change, theological, biblical and liturgical, within
the Church of Rome itself is in many important respects making
Anglicanism look like the more unreformed Church in Ireland. But,
mention should be made of the important contribution which the
Church of Ireland made to the Anglican–Roman Catholic International Commission through the co-chairmanship of Bishop Henry
McAdoo.

George Simms succeeded John Gregg as the most influential bishop in the internal affairs of the Church. It was largely due to him that an entirely new system of appointing bishops was agreed in 1959. Since disestablishment, diocesan synods had appointed their own bishops; now with an electoral college, the wider Church was given a voice in the selection. Beginning with the approval of a new baptism rite, and culminating in the adoption of a modern-language Alternative Prayer Book, both the content and style of worship in the Church of Ireland has been transformed in the latter half of the century. To the regret of many, the use of the Book of Common Prayer is clearly on the wane—though its survival in perhaps a majority of Northern Ireland parishes is just one significant example of how the two parts of the Church of Ireland are beginning to display a quite different ethos.

George Simms also lent his name to proposals for administrative reform, but their lack of success is in part an indication of his own lack of enthusiasm for this area of the Church's life. He was chairman of the committee which produced the radical and far-reaching report *Administration 1967* but his failure to defend its recommendations with any great vigour at Standing Committee and General Synod destroyed any chance which the report had of being adopted.[6] Its main proposals were as follows:

- That the size of the General Synod be reduced from 648 to 501 members.
- That a diocese of Belfast be created and the number of bishops be reduced from fourteen to twelve; this last modest reduction (the much larger Welsh Church has only six bishops) was the only significant recommendation to be adopted.
- That there should be only one cathedral and chapter in each bishopric and that the number of canonries should be reduced.
- That there should only be one diocesan Synod and one diocesan council in each bishopric.
- That there should be four or five properly staffed regional diocesan offices.
- Most significantly of all, the report proposed that there should be three types of parochial units—the traditional incumbency,

6   See the discussion of his role in L. Whiteside, *George Otto Simms*, p. 116.

the pastorate and the chaplaincy. This was an attempt to introduce 'team ministries' and to break down the security of tenure
which inhibits clerical mobility and the best use of clerical man-
power.

• Consequent on the last mentioned proposal was another that clergy
should move to new spheres of work at intervals throughout their
careers.

The almost complete failure of *Administration 67* had the effect of
perpetuating the essentially medieval idea of the parish as a geo-
graphical area within which an incumbent is a solo performer with
unlimited tenure (up to the age of 75) and within which he is frequently also a law unto himself. It, of course, excludes the
development of specialist ministries on which all Churches so much
depend today. The Church of Ireland is largely taken up with the
task of trying to stretch a much-reduced number of full-time clergy
of varying calibre over the traditional parish system; there are now
517. The growing numbers of auxiliary ministers and lay-readers
seem to be regarded mostly as service-takers.

The only administrative area in which some progress can be shown
is the melancholy one of the closing of churches. In the decades
immediately after disestablishment, there was a widespread closing
of churches, most of which had only been built in the first half of the
nineteenth century to avail of the generous government grants which
were made available for church building.[7] Thus, in the extensive
diocese of Lismore, there had been in the eighteenth century only
sixteen places of worship. At disestablishment, this had grown to
thirty-seven, but by 1970 had been reduced to fifteen—almost exactly the number 200 years previously. The Sparsely Populated Areas
Commission (1957–65) was responsible for closing some 144
churches. Seven hundred and forty-three churches were retained in
the rural areas for a population of 55,304. The process has continued in a haphazard manner since then. The retention of particular
places of worship is sadly one of the few things for which the laity

7 *Church building was greatly encouraged* by two Acts of Parliament (43 George
   III Cap 108 and 48 George III Cap 65) which channelled government grants
   through the Board of First Fruits while Acts restraining the building of
   churches in parishes in which no public service had been celebrated for the
   previous twenty years were repealed. This enabled the gentry to have their
   own 'private' churches built largely from public money.

and in particular the rural laity will stand and fight. But the shrink-age of the church network has been an inevitable result of the steady erosion of the Church of Ireland population in most (though not all) areas of the Republic. One of the worst situations revealed by the Sparsely Populated Areas Commission was the diocese of Cashel and Emly where twelve incumbents were to be found ministering to an average of sixty-seven people each. At disestablishment, the Church population in the Twenty six Counties was 338,719; in 1901, 264,264; in 1926, 164,215; in 1961, 104,016; and in 1981, 95,366. The church population of Northern Ireland has not of course fol-lowed the same pattern, but the significance of its size is greatly diminished by the merely nominal nature of so much church mem-bership there. Nonetheless, it now accounts for 78 % of the population of the Church of Ireland, which now stands at 376,838.

I want to end by quoting a remark about the Church of Ireland by the distinguished theologian, Richard Hanson, who tried and failed to be a force for change in the Church of Ireland as bishop of Clogher in the early 1970s. It comes in a review which he wrote of *Irish Anglicanism 1869—1969*, which is a remarkable volume of essays put together by Fr Michael Hurley to celebrate the centenary of disestablishment. Here is what Richard Hanson had to say:

> We are left with a lasting impression of inflexibility and in-elasticity, which hangs around the Church of Ireland. . . . Can the legacy of hatred and prejudice so deeply planted at the grass roots of the Church of Ireland in Ulster be grappled with by daring bishops and clergy ready to lose subscriptions to parishes in the process?

To 'inflexibility', I would want to add 'fearfulness of its ability to survive as a Church'. From that comes fearfulness of any change in the status quo, whether it be numbers of churches in use, or type of liturgy used. Only courageous leadership can deliver from such fears.

Let the last words be Michael Hurley's: 'The Church of Ireland has so far failed to see its destiny as that of a minority Church and therefore it has failed to show the rest of us how to be a minority Church which all Christians must now be—the modern world is at most 30% Christian and 1.5% Anglican'. What I think he means is that we have continued to act as if we were still established—that we don't need to make any great effort to evangelise our lapsed people or to Christianise those we have; an outward conformity is what we are too often prepared to settle for. We have yet as a Church to take to heart some rather uncharacteristic words of Archbishop James McCann to the General Synod of 1966: 'The major issues of evangelisation in a secular and largely non-Christian world completely eclipse the relatively minor subjects debated by our forefathers.' To address these issues and to lead the Church into the twenty-first century will be the task of Archbishop Robert Eames, one of the youngest primates ever at his election in 1986.

SELECT BIBLIOGRAPHY

D.H. Akenson, *The Church of Ireland: 1800–85* (New Haven, 1971)

J.C. Beckett, *A Short History of Ireland* (London, 1952)

D. Bowen, *Superism: Myth or Reality* (Cork, 1970)

—, *The Protestant Crusade in Ireland 1800–70* (Dublin, 1978)

R.R. Hartford, *Godfrey Day* (Dublin, 1940)

Michael Hurley (ed.), *Irish Anglicanism 1969–1969* (Dublin, 1970)

R.B. McDowell, *The Church of Ireland 1869–1969* (London, 1975)

Michael Maher (ed.), *Irish Spirituality* (Dublin, 1981)

K. Milne, *The Church of Ireland: A History* (Dublin, N.D.)

W.G. Neely, *Kilkenny: An Urban History 1391–1843*
    (Belfast, 1989)

W.A. Phillips (ed), *History of the Church of Ireland*, 3 vols.
    (Oxford, 1933)

J.L. Robinson, T.J. Johnston, and R.W. Jackson, *A History of the
    Church of Ireland* (Dublin, 1953)

G. Seaver, *John Gregg, Archbishop* (Dublin, 1963)

Lesley Whiteside, *George Otto Simms* (Gerard's Cross, 1990)

P E N T E C O S T   2

**INTERPRETING
THE LESSONS OF
THE CHURCH YEAR**

LINDA M. MALONEY

**PROCLAMATION 5
SERIES A**

FORTRESS PRESS   MINNEAPOLIS

PROCLAMATION 5
Interpreting the Lessons of the Church Year
Series A, Pentecost 2

Cover and interior design: Spangler Design Team

Library of Congress Cataloging-in-Publication Data
(Revised for vol. [5] thru [8])

Proclamation 5.

    Contents: ser. A. [1] Epiphany / Pheme Perkins —
[2] Holy week / Robert H. Smith — [etc.] — [8] Easter /
David Buttrick.
    1. Bible—Homiletical use.   2. Bible—Liturgical
lessons, English.
BS543.5.P765 1993   251   92-22973
    ISBN 0-8006-4177-9 (ser. A, Advent/Christmas)
    ISBN 0-8006-4178-7 (ser. A, Epiphany)
    ISBN 0-8006-4179-5 (ser. A, Lent)
    ISBN 0-8006-4180-9 (ser. A, Holy week)
    ISBN 0-8006-4181-7 (ser. A, Easter)
    ISBN 0-8006-4182-5 (ser. A, Pentecost 1)
    ISBN 0-8006-4183-3 (ser. A, Pentecost 2)
    ISBN 0-8006-4184-1 (ser. A, Pentecost 3)

The paper used in this publication meets the minimum requirements of American National Standard for Information Sciences—Permanence of Paper for Printed Library Materials, ANSI Z329.48-1984.

∞™

Manufactured in the U.S.A.   AF 1-4183

97   96   95   94   93   1   2   3   4   5   6   7   8   9   10

CONTENTS

Introduction

It is important for the preacher to be aware of the principles of selection underlying modern lectionaries. From the time of the reform of the Roman Lectionary, more than twenty years ago, the usual practice in Ordinary Time (Sundays after Epiphany and after Pentecost) was to select readings according to two criteria: "thematic harmony" and "semicontinuous reading." For the Sundays of Ordinary Time, both New Testament readings are semicontinuous, and the reading from the Jewish Scriptures is chosen to harmonize with the Gospel. Thus the preacher ordinarily has the option of choosing a theme either from the Gospel with its coordinated Old Testament reading, or from the second reading.

The Common Lectionary has introduced a new practice, in response to criticism coming especially from African-American churches that the established practice of typological use of the Old Testament has prevented any kind of semicontinuous reading from those books. As a result, the Common Lectionary substitutes for the typological Old Testament reading a semicontinuous reading of the Pentateuch in the Sundays of Ordinary Time in Year A. Hence the Sundays covered by this volume present a series of readings from Exodus. The preacher using the Common Lectionary has a choice of themes from three semicontinuous readings: Old Testament, apostolic writing, and Gospel.

The "harmony" between Old Testament reading and Gospel is often tenuous at best. In my opinion, the preacher who finds the relationship awkward or inappropriate to the preaching situation is free to develop his or her principal theme from any of the readings individually. Consequently, in the suggestions that follow I have not in all cases drawn tight connections between the first and third readings. I leave that to the creative work of the individual preacher.

My readings are based initially on the text of the New Revised Standard Version, unless otherwise indicated, and ultimately on the texts in their original languages. For further insights, the reader is directed first to the excellent one-volume Bible commentaries now available, such as *Harper's Bible Commentary*, J. L. Mays, ed. (San Francisco: Harper & Row, 1988) and *The New Jerome Bible Commentary* (Englewood Cliffs, N.J.: Prentice-Hall, 1990), especially the fine article on Romans by Joseph Fitzmyer (pp. 830–68). For important new insights, see also Carol A. Newsom and Sharon H. Ringe, eds., *The Women's Bible Commentary* (Louisville: Westminster/John Knox, 1992). The best multivolume commentaries on Romans and on these chapters of Matthew are still in German, but I have benefited by the insights of Daniel J. Harrington, S.J., *The Gospel of Matthew*, Sacra Pagina 1 (Collegeville, Minn.: Liturgical Press/Michael Glazier, 1991). For the parables, a newer book that will be very useful to preachers is by John R. Donahue, S.J., *The Gospel in Parable* (Philadelphia: Fortress Press, 1988). All these works offer short bibliographies that, due to the recent publication dates, are good guides to some of the newest books and articles.

For the Old Testament readings I have consulted a variety of sources, but for further reference I would like to recommend especially Michael D. Guinan, *The Pentateuch*, Message of Biblical Spirituality 1 (Collegeville, Minn.: Liturgical Press, 1990), and Ralph W. Klein, *Ezekiel: The Prophet and His Message* (Columbia: Univ. of South Carolina Press, 1988). I am at all times indebted to my teacher, Gerhard Lohfink, for New Testament insights, and to Norbert Lohfink for stimulating ideas on the Old Testament. I enthusiastically recommend any and all of their many books.

My thanks are due to the patient editors at Fortress Press and to the exceptional library of the Graduate Theological Union in Berkeley, California and its librarians. I might have wished that the library's temporary closing for the installation of the electronic circulation system had not coincided with the last days preceding the completion of this book—but without the use of its invaluable collection I could not have considered undertaking the project at all. Much of the credit for the book's excellences belongs to them; its faults are entirely my own.

Tenth Sunday after Pentecost

Lutheran	Roman Catholic	Episcopal	Common Lectionary
1 Kings 3:5-12	1 Kings 3:5, 7-12	1 Kings 3:5-12	Exod. 3:13-20
Rom. 8:28-30	Rom. 8:28-30	Rom. 8:26-34	Rom. 8:26-30
Matt. 13:44-52	Matt. 13:44-52	Matt. 13:31-33, 44-49a	Matt. 13:44-52

FIRST LESSON: 1 KINGS 3:5-12

The first book of Kings begins with the old age of King David, the choice of his successor, and David's death. With chapter 3, the reign of David's son Solomon begins. Like so many auspicious careers in Scripture, it starts with a dream, recounted in 1 Kings 3:5-15.

Before this, however, we have been given some important information that will tie in with later events. The account of Solomon's reign is written as a kind of "ring composition" or series of concentric narratives. Events of the beginning are repeated at the end, or early details presage things to come.

Thus, at the beginning of chapter 3, we read of Solomon's first marriage, to a daughter of Pharaoh (3:1), and of his worshiping and sacrificing, as did all the people of Israel, "at the high places," because no house had yet been built for the Lord in Jerusalem. The worship of God only in the Jerusalem Temple is a concern of the Deuteronomic authors of this history, and although it is obviously excusable to worship elsewhere when no temple exists, there is still a hint of foreboding in this fact—as there is in the first of Solomon's foreign marriages—because we learn later that (according to the authors) it is his foreign wives who will lead Solomon away from the proper path and cause him once again to worship and sacrifice at the high places, even though by this time he has built a house for the Lord in Jerusalem (11:1-13). This kind of scapegoating of women characters in the story reaches its ultimate climax in the stories about Jezebel in 2 Kings.

The need to worship at one of the high places, because there is as yet no temple in Jerusalem, excuses Solomon's going to Gibeon to sacrifice. Afterward, YHWH appears to Solomon in a dream. This kind of event is known as "incubation dreaming." In these incidents, a person sleeps in the sanctuary in order to receive a message from a deity, as Solomon does here. We are familiar with other similar scenes in the Old Testament: for example, Jacob's dream at Bethel in Genesis 28, or Samuel's dream in 1 Samuel 3. In Egyptian texts we often find that a Pharaoh who is about to introduce significant innovations first receives an authorizing dream. It frequently happens that the dreamer is allowed to ask a favor, and so it is here. Solomon's response refers to past, present, and future: to the past relationship between YHWH and David, to Solomon's accession to David's throne in accordance with the promise, and to Solomon's future governance. His request has to do with that future, for Solomon asks for the ability to govern wisely.

Solomon's request is approved: YHWH grants him wisdom beyond all others, but also the riches and power he did not ask for. In the scene immediately following, Solomon is given a chance to demonstrate his wisdom by settling the dispute between two women over a child each claims is hers.

The scene with the two women is a reminder of an important aspect of the motif of wisdom in the wisdom literature of the Jewish Scriptures, which took Solomon as its prototype of the wise person. That is the juxtaposition of Woman Wisdom with Woman Folly. It is no accident that Solomon's reception of wisdom is followed by an illustration of the application of wisdom couched in the form of a dispute between two women. In spite of his disclaimer, Solomon has received both a wise and discerning mind and the gifts of riches and power; however, the first gift must control the others if Solomon is truly to rule wisely over God's chosen people. As it turns out, although he gives the "wise" judgment in the first case, Solomon is ultimately seduced by riches, power, and even religious syncretism portrayed in terms of his foreign wives; though his own reign is prosperous, the sequel will be disaster.

In another dimension, the wisdom versus folly struggle reflects and reverses the events of 2 Samuel 11–12. Despite the praise heaped on David in 1 Kings 3:6 (a passage added by the Deuteronomic editor; see the parallel passage in 2 Chron. 1:3-13), the structure and language of the passage show that here Solomon is reversing the action of his father, David. David chose folly by seducing Bathsheba, Solomon's mother, and murdering her husband; the result was the death of the couple's first child and a curse on David's house. Now Solomon chooses wisdom and exercises right judgment: The result is a living child and a blessing on Solomon's house. (For this interpretation, see Carole Fontaine, "The Bearing of Wisdom on the Shape of 2 Samuel 11–12 and 1 Kings 3," *Journal for the Study of the Old Testament* 34 [1986]: 61–77, and the summary in Claudia V. Camp, "1 and 2 Kings," *The Women's Bible Commentary*, 100–1.)

ALTERNATIVE FIRST LESSON: EXODUS 3:13-20

The reading from Exodus is an excerpt from the commissioning of Moses. The first part of the passage is from the Elohist source (E); according to that writer, the divine name YHWH is first revealed at this point. There is a sharp caesura between past and future. Israel's God, formerly known to them only as the god of the ancestors, takes the additional, intimate step of revealing a personal name; it is this name by which future generations in Israel are to call on their God. In this sense, the giving of the name constitutes a commitment on God's part to be a participant in this people's history from now on. Eventually, that name came to be regarded as so awesomely sacred that it was not to be pronounced, and when the Scriptures were read aloud the Hebrew word *adonai* or Greek *kyrios* ("Lord") was substituted for the word represented by the four consonants YHWH. This had the unfortunate effect of masculinizing the name, because "Lord" is generally understood as a masculine reference, while the mysterious name represented by the tetragrammaton YHWH does not in itself imply any gender or sexuality.

The meaning of the Hebrew word is obscure. It is most probably derived from the verb "to be" and thus means something like "I am who I am," or "I will be who I will be." Some scholars think it is an attenuated form of another identification, "(God who) creates (the heavenly host)" (so, for example, Brevard Childs, *The Book of Exodus* [Philadelphia: Westminster, 1974], 60–64). In any case, it expresses the freedom and the mystery of this God.

According to the Yahwist source (J), on the other hand, this name of God had been known to the ancestors from the beginning; it thus appears as the name of the creator in Genesis 2. In our passage, J takes up the story at 3:16, repeating the identification of YHWH ("the LORD") with the god of the ancestors. Whether Israel did not yet know the name of their God (E), or had forgotten it and needed reminding (J), God is commissioning a prophet to speak to them and to reveal God's plan for their liberation. God never acts without prophetic revelation, according to Amos 3:7. Israel is to pass from the control of Pharaoh to that of their own God, whose plan for them is freedom, breadth, and richness.

The passage may serve us as a guide in our own struggle to discern the true path to human liberation. If we want to know God's plan, we must first recognize God's prophets. Of those who come before us as prophets, we should first ask the name—the true name—of the God they serve. If we are satisfied that they are genuine prophets of the one God who wills the good of all people and of all creation, we may ask them what knowledge of or insight into the divine plan has been given to them. We should be neither too easily dismissive of the prophets, nor too easily led by those whose offers are alluring, but who do not know the name of the god they serve.

SECOND LESSON: ROMANS 8:26-34

The continuous reading from Paul's letter to the Christians at Rome here reaches the climax of a section that began with 5:1. The theme of the section is the love of God, which assures salvation to all who have been justified by faith. (See Joseph Fitzmyer, "Romans," *The New Jerome Biblical Commentary*, 830-68.) The Christians' destiny—a glorious life in the Spirit, beyond all threat of change or decay—is attested, in the first place, by creation, which struggles toward that end; secondly, by the longing of our own human spirit; and finally, by the Spirit of God, who comes to the aid of human strivings. It is the intercession of the Spirit (here described in language drawn from the law courts, reminiscent of the Paraclete sayings in the Johannine corpus, and of the Gospel assurances in Mark 13:11; Matt. 10:19-20; and Luke 21:15) that clinches the argument. God searches human hearts (an expression drawn from the OT: cf. 1 Sam. 16:7; 1 Kings 8:39; Pss. 7:11; 17:3; 139:1), but it is God alone who knows the mind of the Spirit and can respond to the Spirit's pleadings on behalf of humankind. The Spirit can even make use of our wordless and inarticulate longings and turn them into eloquent pleas. (See John A. T. Robinson, *Wrestling with Romans* [London: SCM, 1979], 104.)

Verses 28-30 are a concise description of the divine plan for salvation, apparently relying on a traditional confession drawn from the wisdom tradition. Paul is thinking in corporate terms of all who respond to the divine call: The application of this language to individual predestination stems from the later interpretation of Augustine. There is a problem in translating the Greek: It may either mean that God cooperates in all things for good with those who love God, or that, (as in NRSV), "all things work together for good" for those who love God. In either case, Paul certainly means to say that the movement of all things toward a good end is part of God's plan.

With verse 31, Paul begins a rhetorical climax rising to hymnic heights. Elements of the diatribe and the terminology of the court return, with references to judgment, condemnation, and intercession. There may be an allusion to Gen. 22:16 and Abraham's willingness to sacrifice his son, Isaac; God will not be outdone by Abraham in generosity. Different punctuation of this passage yields slightly different rhythm and rhetoric; some translations have a series of rhetorical questions: "Who shall bring any charge against God's elect? Is it God who justifies? Who is to condemn? Is it Christ Jesus, . . ." The RSV and NRSV have, instead, "It is God who justifies. Who is to condemn?" This relies on a reference to Isa. 50:8-9, but seems to break the rhythmic flow of the argument and the correspondence with the following passage. In either case, the argument is clear: God, who has already given so much for human beings, is certainly not going to turn and condemn them.

An important theme of this whole section is divine impartiality. We should not read this simply to mean that God is evenhanded or, worse, indifferent. On the contrary: It means that God does not use the same yardstick as human beings do. We are never impartial; in our judgments and interpretations, interests are always at work, whether we are conscious of them or not. God, on the other hand, has no preference for any individual or group. God does not prefer men to women, the rich to the poor, even the industrious to the lazy. God never judges by wealth or position, nor even by behavior, for God searches human hearts and hears the cries of the Spirit on our behalf.

In the context of the whole chapter, also, it is worth noting that God's call is extended not merely to human beings but to the whole creation, and that Christ's sacrifice is in that sense "cosmic." The "groaning" of creation in travail, its anxious expectation of the future glory, is a sign that when God "give[s] us all things with [God's Son]," this means that all things are entrusted to us for the good of all (cf. Gen. 1:28), not that they are handed over for our exploitation. Martin Luther already saw this point in his commentary on Romans; it has become a burning issue for us at the end of the twentieth century.

GOSPEL: MATTHEW 13:44-52

This reading includes several groups of selections from the "parables discourse" in Matthew. The parables of the mustard seed and the leaven have in common the theme "great results from small beginnings," while the parables of the treasure in the field and the pearl of great price concern the necessity of abandoning everything lesser to gain the one real treasure: the realm of God. Finally, the parable of the net concerns the gathering of all, good and bad, into one society, even one church, in the here and now; only at the end of all things will a division be made. The disciples in Matthew (unlike the disciples in Mark's Gospel) understand the parables. The discourse ends with a saying about "every scribe who is trained for the realm of heaven," which some commentators see as a signature note by the author of this Gospel. Whether that is the case or not, it is the task of such a person to steward the community's treasure, its tradition, and to draw out and apply the different parts of that teaching—including the Old Testament and the new Christian traditions—as they are needed by the community in the different circumstances of its life.

The mustard seed and the leaven parables conclude Jesus' "public" discourse; the other three are addressed only to the disciples. Two details of the mustard seed parable mark Matthew's version as different from Mark's. In the first place, Mark simply speaks of the seed being "sown upon the ground" (Mark 4:31), not necessarily the work of a conscious agent, while in Matthew's version "someone took [it] and sowed it in his field," two quite deliberate steps. In the second place, Mark speaks of the seed growing into "the greatest of all shrubs, [with] large branches, so that the birds of the air can make nests in its shade" (4:32). In Matthew, it "becomes a tree, so that the birds of the air come and make nests in its branches." Mark's emphasis (and probably Jesus') lies on the surprising comparison of the reign of God with a tiny, common seed; Matthew's stress shifts attention to the "tree," a familiar metaphor for eschatological fulfillment. The Matthean community is encouraged to think that their tiny group is the seed of the great tree to which the "birds" (often a metaphor for Gentiles) will flock.

The parable of the mustard seed is balanced, in Matthew's and Luke's Gospels, by another such story drawn from their other common source, apparently a collection of Jesus sayings. The two taken together illustrate the division of labor between men and women: the man in the field, the woman in the house. Again something relatively obscure, the yeast (really "sourdough"), is mixed with (literally "hidden in") three measures of flour—a very large amount, about a bushel, or, in other words, as much flour as one woman could possibly knead at one time, producing roughly 100 pounds of bread, enough to feed more than one hundred people. Again the comparison would have surprised Jesus' hearers. Most often in Scripture, we encounter leaven as representative of a kind of impurity that has to be purged from the household or the spiritual body (cf. Matt. 16:6, 11-12 and parallels; 1 Cor. 5:7); here, though, it is the one thing necessary, together with the woman's labor, to produce the wonderful effect: the bread of life.

The parables of the treasure in the field and the pearl merchant are linked with the mustard seed parable by the catchword "field," and with the yeast parable by the topos of hiddenness. They have a common element of joyful surprise, although in the first case the finding seems to be fortuitous, while in the second it is the result of a deliberate and painstaking search. One thing that both have in common with the first reading is the exercise of wisdom. To stake everything on buying a field or a single pearl may seem foolhardy on the face of it, but the reward is far greater than the price; and so it is when it comes to seeking the reign of God. No obstacle should hinder us in that quest, and surely it is to be prized above riches: It is beyond price.

We should take note of the fact that the parable of the treasure in the field features one of Jesus' "immoral" heroes. (See J. D. Crossan, *Finding Is the First Act: Trove Folktales and Jesus' Treasure Parable* [Philadelphia: Fortress Press, 1979].) These two "finding" stories did not originally belong together; they do not represent a pairing of a story of a poor person with one about a rich person, to match the pairing of male and female activities in the mustard seed and the leaven. The person who finds the treasure is not "poor but deserving," since he (or she) can, by selling everything, raise enough money to buy the field. No notice is given to the owner of the field that a treasure has been found there. The lucky finder simply buys the field and keeps the goods. This may be a legal action, but it is hardly moral. As Crossan notes, "*If the treasure belongs to the finder, buying the land is unnecessary. But, if the treasure does not belong to the finder, buying the land is unjust*" (*Finding Is the First Act*, 91. Italics in original.)

Only if we plumb the full import of the situation are we able to appreciate the impact of the parable. The finder of the treasure lives the injunction of the Sermon on the Mount, to take no thought for tomorrow, quite literally, because once he or she has sold everything to buy the field, there is no tomorrow: Nothing is left to sell except the treasure, and that would be the opposite of the finder's intention. The point of the parable is not to teach good morals. It is simply that in order to obtain the treasure that is the reign of God, one must act immediately and not count the cost.

The last parable, that of the net, parallels and balances the parable of the weeds in vv. 24-30. The point of each of them is that Christians should not worry about trying to weed out the bad members of society or the "misfits" in the Christian body. God will take care of that, at the end of all things. The sorting out belongs to God; the Christian's task is forbearance and forgiveness.

The person who understands these parables and acts accordingly will be wise, like Solomon, in seeking the one thing that is necessary. Riches, power, and long life are auxiliary benefits that may accrue; the one important thing is to "seek first God's reign and God's justice" (Matt. 6:33).

Eleventh Sunday after Pentecost

Lutheran	Roman Catholic	Episcopal	Common Lectionary
Isa. 55:1-5	Isa. 55:1-3	Neh. 9:16-20	Exod. 12:1-14
Rom. 8:35-39	Rom. 8:35, 37-39	Rom. 8:35-39	Rom. 8:31-39
Matt. 14:13-21	Matt. 14:13-21	Matt. 14:13-21	Matt. 14:13-21

FIRST LESSON: ISAIAH 55:1-5

This reading contains an excerpt from the hymn at the end of Deutero-Isaiah's vision of the return of the exiles of Israel. It was undoubtedly chosen for this Sunday's reading because of the food and banqueting theme, relating to the Gospel reading, the feeding of the multitude.

The genre of the text is that of a divine invitation to a banquet, similar to those in Proverbs 9 and Sirach 24. Wisdom, in Proverbs, invites: "Come, eat of my bread and drink of the wine I have mixed. Lay aside immaturity, and live, and walk in the way of insight"; in Sirach she cries: "Those who eat me will hunger for more, and those who drink me will thirst for more. Whoever obeys me will not be put to shame . . ." (Prov. 9:5-6; Sir. 24:21-22). In the longer passage from Isaiah, also, the invitation to leave aside folly is implicit in v. 2, and explicit in vv. 7-8.

We are once again in the realm of Wisdom. In the previous week's first reading, we heard of Solomon's choice of wisdom. Ultimately, however, Solomon turned to folly. Now, at the end of the exile, there is a new beginning in which the task of witnessing, of speaking wisely, formerly the duty of king or prophet, is transferred to the whole people. The covenant is now offered anew to Israel as a whole; it is Israel that will call the foreign nations, and they will come, blinded by the glory bestowed on Israel by its God. (See Ralph W. Klein, *Israel in Exile: A Theological Interpretation* [Philadelphia: Fortress Press, 1979], 119–21.)

In the larger context of the book, Isaiah 54 gave a poetic account of the building of the new Temple at the end of the exile. On such an occasion, there would be a great banquet: Chapter 55 is the invitation to that feast. Because there is repeated reference to an "everlasting covenant," and to the pilgrimage of nations to Zion, we cannot fail to hear the overtones of an invitation to the eschatological, messianic banquet as well.

The "non-bread" and unsatisfying food in v. 2 are—in contrast to the banquet of Wisdom or Messiah—the things we gain for ourselves by our own efforts, spending our wages, the fruit of our toil. The text here speaks in a spirit akin to that of the Sermon on the Mount: The birds of the air, who depend entirely on God, are better fed than we. The very brief reformulation of the covenant in vv. 3-5 hints at a related understanding of the complementary image of the "lilies of the field." The glory in which they are arrayed, greater than that of Solomon, is the glory God bestows on God's faithful people—just as, here, the covenant with David is extended to the whole nation and becomes their glory.

ALTERNATIVE FIRST LESSON: NEHEMIAH 9:16-20

Like the reading from Isaiah, this passage from Nehemiah belongs within the context of return from exile and the rebuilding of the Temple. In the Hebrew text, it is a confessional prayer placed in the mouth of the Levites, extending from vv. 5b-37. The Greek text attributes it to Ezra, as part of his proclamation of the Torah. Although this "prayer of the Levites" was not preserved as such in the synagogue after Ezra, it deeply influenced the structure of the synagogue's liturgy, and thus (probably by way of the synagogue) the Christian Eucharist.

The text stresses that God's promise is not thwarted even by Israel's unfaithfulness. When the people wanted to turn back in the wilderness and return to bondage in Egypt, God's response was to renew and redouble the gifts already given. God's patience outlasts human impatience.

This confession belongs to the special form called the *tōdā*, the thanksgiving of a person released from suffering or bondage. When the thanksgiving sacrifice was brought to the Temple, the person who had been healed or delivered recited the story of the events: the suffering, the anguish, the divine action of release. Some scholars have suggested that the *tōdā* was *a* model, if not *the* model, for the Christian Eucharist, with its anamnesis (memorial recitation) of the life, death, and resurrection of Jesus the Christ.

There are a number of elements, then, in the reading that make it an appropriate companion to Matthew's account of the feeding of five thousand: the liturgical, and especially eucharistic associations, the account of Israel's being "in the wilderness," and the reference to God's gift of manna. In both instances, the people's natural hunger and thirst are satisfied as such, and on a higher plane as well, by God's perfect gift.

ALTERNATIVE FIRST LESSON: EXODUS 12:1-14

This section of Exodus is taken from the Priestly source. It describes the rite of the Passover lamb, and is followed immediately, in vv. 14-20, by the description of the rite of unleavened bread. Originally, the two rituals were separate; Israel celebrated them consecutively, with the one-day feast of Passover followed by the fifteen days of unleavened bread. A brief reference to the unleavened bread has been inserted into the Passover ritual account (v. 8); the author combines the two rituals and inserts them within the account of the tenth plague, the death of the firstborn, between the announcement of the plague and its fulfillment.

The beginning of the account proclaims a new calendar, reflecting the time period and perspective of the Priestly writer. During the monarchy, Israel's year began with the fall harvest (cf. Exod. 23:16; 34:22). When exiled to Babylon, the Israelites adopted the Babylonian calendar, which began in the spring of the year, and they continued to use that calendar even after the exile. Thus the month of Abib (March–April) is here declared to be "the first month of the year for you." This fits well with the ancient nomadic feast of Passover, in which a young animal was slaughtered and its blood smeared on the doorposts (or tent poles) as a talisman against any evil that might attack the flock. It is less appropriate for the feast of unleavened bread, when the leaven derived from the previous year's grain harvest was purged and replaced with new.

Whether in spring or fall, however, each of these feasts celebrates a transition from old to new; the image of the journey emphasizes that the old is being left behind. Because they are going on a journey, the participants wear the clothing of travelers. None of the food they are to eat uses the products of the old culture or of the old year: no cooking pots or water for boiling, because the animal is to be roasted whole in the fire; no old leaven, apparently no cultivated herb. (The identity of the "bitter herbs" is not clear, but quite possibly they are some kind of naturally occurring weeds.) The food has not been altered by human culture (e.g., by boiling or fermenting); it is the kind of "pure" food that is fit to be offered in sacrifice, and that purifies those who partake of it. The Priestly author differs from the Deuteronomist in two ways: First, according to P, the sacrifice belongs to the households and is not to be carried out at a central sanctuary; second, the Deuteronomist orders that the animal be boiled (Deut. 16:7), but P, in prescribing that it be roasted in the fire, probably reflects the more ancient custom.

The blood rite mentioned in vv. 7 and 13 may retain some maternal symbolism, because its imagery suggests the birth passage. It was combined at an early stage with the sacrifice of the lamb. It may be this sacrifice to which Moses repeatedly refers in his conversations with Pharaoh (cf. Exod. 3:18 and elsewhere). As it now stands, the whole combined ritual reflects a stage at which the destroyer of the flock has become a threat to the firstborn of all mammalian life, most importantly the human.

Because this is a semicontinuous reading, the connection with Jesus' feeding of the multitude "in the wilderness" is only accidental, and tenuous at best. John's Gospel does associate the feeding miracle with Passover and its symbolism, but that is not the case in Matthew.

SECOND LESSON: ROMANS 8:35-39

(For commentary on verses 31-34, see the reading for the previous Sunday.)

The last verses of chapter 8 constitute the hymnic high point and conclusion to this section of Romans that began at 5:1. Paul hammers home the point:

Those whom God has called, and who have responded by joining themselves to Christ, conforming themselves to Christ's image, can never again be torn from the love of Christ (that is, Christ's love for us), because (referring to v. 34) Christ is at the right hand of God and exercises God's power on our behalf.

Paul rarely speaks of Christ's love for us (only here and 2 Cor. 5:14-15; Gal. 2:20). On Paul's lips, the phrase always means the loving self-gift of Christ on our behalf. In Christ's love we witness the love of God at work and—to complete the trinitarian picture—the fullness of that love is realized for us in the gift of the Spirit (cf. Rom. 15:30) made possible by Christ's self-surrender on the cross.

In verse 35, Paul lists the very sufferings he himself has undergone for the sake of the gospel: There are seven, culminating in the sword, that is, death itself, which he has not yet experienced but expects to meet in some such form. It is doubtful that these trials have yet visited the church at Rome. There follows a quotation from Ps. 44:22 (23), taken word for word from the Greek Old Testament: "Because of you we are being killed all day long, and accounted as sheep for the slaughter." In its original context, this is a lament, prefacing a cry to God for help. Here Paul uses it to make the point that tribulation is itself the mark of our belonging to God. It is "because of" or "for the sake of" God that we are suffering, just as Jesus before us suffered for his allegiance to God, and thereby won the victory for all of us. Hence we are "more than conquerors" through the one who loved us—which may refer either to Christ or to God.

The next two verses contain a list of ten adversaries or transpersonal powers, all created things, none of which has the strength or the ability to separate us from the love of God that is ours in and through Jesus, who because of his steadfast fidelity is Christ and Lord. The juxtaposition of paired concepts occasionally leads to a puzzling presentation, as when "life" is coupled with "death" as something threatening. It may be that Paul is thinking of those aspects of this life that could distract us and lead us away from the way of Christ (cf. Mark 4:19 and parallels). "Angels," "principalities," and "powers" are supernatural beings of different ranks, and can be good or evil. The things of the present are threatening enough, but we have no idea of the trials to come; still, we should not be anxious. "Height" and "depth" may be astrological references, personified extremes. None of these, no imaginable thing in creation, has the power to divide us from God in Christ.

GOSPEL: MATTHEW 14:13-21

The account of the feeding of five thousand men (plus women and children) is found in all three of the Synoptic Gospels, as well as in John; Mark and Matthew also contain a second account of the feeding of four thousand (plus). The multiple attestations of the story do not necessarily or even probably mean that it was an historical event, but they certainly indicate that it had an extraordinary significance for the early Christian community.

In Matthew's version, the event immediately preceding this one is the beheading of John the Baptizer. Strong, ironic parallels are drawn between the two episodes: Herod's banquet versus Jesus' banquet; Herodias and her daughter at Herod's feast versus the women and children at Jesus' feast; John's head on a dish and Jesus' distributing of bread to the seated multitude.

Matthew's drama takes place in three acts: the exposition in vv. 13-14, which in itself has nothing to do with the feeding; a dialogue between Jesus and the disciples (the central focus of Matthew's account); and the miracle itself. Verse 21 is a parenthetic remark by the narrator. Matthew has made some typical alterations in Mark's version of events. While Mark reports that Jesus was teaching the people, Matthew tells us that he was healing the sick. Matthew also continues the process of "rehabilitating" the disciples, who are so negatively portrayed in Mark. While in Mark's account the disciples argue with Jesus about the sheer impossibility of buying enough bread to feed so many people, in Matthew Jesus puts the matter to them straightforwardly: "They need not go away; you give them something to eat." The disciples do not quibble—after all, like Peter in the next story and like the Matthean community, they have at least "a little faith." They simply state the condition of the larder: five loaves and two fish. There is not much point in trying to manufacture a symbolism for the fish. They seem to be a fixed element in the story, even though they do not correspond to the eucharistic symbolism that pervades the gospel accounts. In fact, bread and salted or pickled fish were the standard fare of poor people, in Galilee and elsewhere, in the first century.

In Matthew's version, it is the disciples who distribute the loaves (no mention is made of the fish) to the crowds; they are the mediators of Jesus' action, as befitting their role in the Matthean church. The crowds are told to "recline" (not merely to "sit down") on the grass. There is a subtle significance in this: In the ancient world, common meals were taken sitting, or even standing, but at a feast or a banquet, the people reclined on couches, symbolizing freedom and leisure. Here, at Jesus' banquet, even though it takes place in an open field and not in a banquet hall, the people (men, women, and children) are told to recline like the free and noble persons they are. They are people of great dignity, because they are the restored Israel gathered and fed by Jesus, the Messiah.

The number of the people emphasizes this last point. We learn that there are five thousand men "besides women and children." Demographically speaking, if the numbers are representative of their proportions in the population, these three groups together could well add up to twenty or thirty thousand people, something like ten percent of the entire population of Palestine! They are a "representative tenth" of all Israel. Continuing the identification with the Jewish people, Jesus praises God and distributes the food like the presider at a Jewish meal, and the language and elements of the story echo the history of and promises to Israel. Thus "they all ate and were filled [or satisfied]" like the people in Isa. 55:1-3, and there are strong echoes of the miracles of manna and quail in Exodus 16 and Numbers 11 (when the people were fed "in the wilderness" [erēmos], just as they are here), and of Elisha's feeding of one hundred men with twenty loaves in 2 Kings 4:1-7, 42-44.

The whole passage contains two levels of symbolism: from mundane bread to satisfy daily hunger to the bread of the Eucharist to satisfy the hunger of the spirit; and from the daily bread of the Eucharist to the messianic banquet in the reign of God. Nevertheless, the eucharistic element should not be overemphasized. Rather, this is, on a grand scale, one of those meals that Jesus, during his earthly life, so gladly shared with people of all kinds. It points forward to his presence, after Easter, among those who celebrate the eucharistic memorial, but it can only do so because it is embedded in the context of many meals shared.

Twelfth Sunday after Pentecost

Lutheran	Roman Catholic	Episcopal	Common Lectionary
1 Kings 19:9-18	1 Kings 19:9a, 11-13a	Jon. 2:1-9	Exod. 14:19-31
Rom. 9:1-5	Rom. 9:1-5	Rom. 9:1-5	Rom. 9:1-5
Matt. 14:22-33	Matt. 14:22-33	Matt. 14:22-33	Matt. 14:22-33

FIRST LESSON: 1 KINGS 19:9-18

In the story of the prophet Elijah, there comes a time when Elijah flees in terror from the power of Queen Jezebel (19:3). Elijah is so dejected that he no longer wants to live, but an angel of the Lord rouses him and sends him on his way to Mount Horeb, where the incident recounted in 19:9-18 takes place.

There is much in the story that parallels the career of Moses, and there can be no doubt that the author of 1 Kings wants to portray Elijah as a prophet like Moses. The journey of forty days and forty nights reflects Moses' sojourn on the mountain (called Sinai in the southern, Judahite literature, but Horeb in the traditions of the north). The "cave" in which Elijah is hidden is like the "cleft of the rock" in which Moses stood (Exod. 33:22) when YHWH "passed by" (Exod. 33:19-23), as also happens in 1 Kings 19:11. In addition, the wind, earthquake, and fire repeat the events of the Sinai theophany as told in Exodus 19.

Beyond these specifics, Elijah's journey is couched in terms of a pilgrimage to a sacred place, in which the pilgrim leaves food and companionship behind and undertakes a solitary journey. The whole section is shaped by a question (from YHWH), a complaint (by Elijah), and a command (by YHWH): The pattern is repeated twice. Each time, YHWH's question is the same: "What are you doing *here*, Elijah?" Where should Elijah be? In Israel, of course, carrying out his prophetic duties. Nevertheless, he has some problems with that, as he forcefully explains: Although he himself has faithfully served YHWH, the people of Israel have not. They have abandoned the covenant, thrown down YHWH's altars, and put the prophets to the sword. Elijah is the only prophet left, and he has no ambition to join the others.

YHWH responds by commanding Elijah to "go out and stand on the mountain before YHWH." Apparently Elijah does not immediately do so. Like Moses, he remains hidden while the violent theophany is raging—only this time it turns into a kind of antitheophany, because the text tells us that YHWH is not in the wind, or in the earthquake, or in the fire. Is this a deliberate rejection, because of the danger of syncretism, of the storm theophany that had been part of the religion of YHWH (as reflected in the Sinai traditions)? Such theophanies had a special association with Baal, the primary adversary of YHWH and YHWH's prophets in Israel. Whether this is a deliberate attack on storm theophanies or not, it certainly marks a change from spectacular divine appearances to the quiet transmission of YHWH's word to and through the prophets, for what ultimately triggers Elijah's belated, obedient response is a "sound of sheer silence." (This more accurate translation has a great deal to recommend it, especially because it points up the mysterious nature of the sound, as opposed to anthropomorphizing and even trivializing expressions such as "a still small voice" or "a tiny whispering sound.")

So the second cycle begins: Elijah finally obeys the first command, and is immediately confronted with the repeated question: "What are you doing *here*, Elijah?" Obstinately, Elijah repeats, word for word, his objection to being killed, but YHWH is not taking "no" for an answer. This time the command is more far-reaching: "Go, return on your way . . ." The commission that follows answers Elijah's objections in detail: Elijah is to anoint new kings for Syria and Israel to replace the Baal worshipers, and a successor prophet in the person of Elisha. Finally, YHWH denies Elijah's assertion that he is the only faithful worshiper of YHWH left in Israel: There are seven thousand more, and these will be spared in the general slaughter to form the core of a new Israel for YHWH. "Seven thousand" is symbolic: It represents a large number, sufficient to form the requisite basis for the renewed people.

To believe, to hope, to follow YHWH's plan, even when it is not expressed in obvious events or proclamations, but only in "a sound of sheer silence," these should be the guidelines for all those who fear and follow the true God.

ALTERNATIVE FIRST LESSON: JONAH 2:1-9 (2-10)

The reading presents Jonah's psalm of thanksgiving, cut out of its context. The previous verse had told how "the Lord provided a large fish to swallow up Jonah, and Jonah was in the belly of the fish three days and three nights," and the immediate sequel to the psalm is "then the Lord spoke to the fish, and it spewed Jonah out upon the dry land." Presumably Jonah's psalm was chosen for today's reading because it describes the situation of someone "cast . . . into the deep," in distress at sea, sinking and crying out to the Lord for assistance.

This is, in fact, a classic song of thanksgiving like many of the psalms of the Old Testament. It consists of a narrative of distress, a notice that the sufferer has cried to God for help, and a narration of God's response. In fact, it is a *tōdā* psalm. It is couched in terms of Semitic mythology, in which death, or the approach to death, was often described as entry into the underworld or a sinking in cosmic waters (cf. Pss. 69 and 88, in particular). Three days and three nights were the standard period required for a descent to the underworld.

21

The problem is that this psalm, lovely in itself, is so out of place in its context. Perhaps it only calls our attention in the strongest way to the arrogance and stubbornness of this "antiprophet." Jonah has, after all, refused the divine command and tried to flee. How can he say, "I called to the Lord out of my distress," when in fact the only people who have been calling on the Lord, up to this time, are the crew of the ship who finally, and reluctantly, cast Jonah into the sea? How can he say to the Lord, "you cast me into the deep," when it was the sailors who did so? What does Jonah care about looking again on the Lord's temple, when he was trying to get as far from it as possible? Finally, who is he maligning as "those who worship vain idols"? The sailors, who "feared the Lord even more, and . . . offered a sacrifice to the Lord and made vows" (1:16) after seeing the waves stop raging? or the poor people of Nineveh, to whom Jonah has declined to bring the message of warning? In fact, Jonah's reaction to YHWH's command stands, throughout the book, as an ironic counterpoint to the behavior of the Ninevites, who, once they have been warned, immediately repent and do penance: The result of that is that they are reprieved, and Jonah, far from rejoicing at the outcome, is mortally peeved! The only line of Jonah's psalm that rings completely true is the last one: "Deliverance belongs to the LORD!"

Ultimately, as Phyllis Trible has observed, it is no wonder that Jonah made the fish sick to its stomach! The psalm, at the center of the book, is also its crowning irony. Jonah is a great one to "talk the talk," for he mouths pious phrases throughout the book. His problem is that he is unwilling to "walk the walk," to act in consequence of his stated beliefs. His situation is, in a certain sense, the reverse of Peter's in the gospel. Peter's problem is his "little faith." He tests that faith too far in attempting to "walk the walk" over the sea, and has to cry out for help. Jonah, on the other hand, has abundant faith—at least if we can believe his talk—but as for *going* anywhere with it, he says, "Thanks, but no thanks." Surely the world is better off with the Simon Peters who try and fail than with the Jonahs who are content just to be.

ALTERNATIVE FIRST LESSON: EXODUS 14:19-31

A third pericope offered for the first reading of this Sunday also (coincidentally) has to do with divine action at the sea; in this case, it is the Sea of Reeds, where Israel was delivered from Egypt.

The pericope contains material primarily from the Yahwist and Priestly sources, with a few notes added by the Elohist writer. Each source conceives the battle differently: The earlier Yahwist source saw the whole episode as a divine action, in which the storm god drove back the sea throughout the night, while Israel crossed over; in the morning the sea returned to its normal depth. In the ancient hymn that follows (Exod. 15:1-18), YHWH's storm capsizes the Egyptians' boats. For the Priestly writer, Moses acts as God's agent in the moving of the sea: Moses divides the sea with a rod so that Israel can walk through on dry land; when Israel has crossed over, Moses raises his hand and the walls of water crash down on the Egyptian army.

The note that the Egyptian army was destroyed "at the morning watch" (which may have influenced Matt. 14:25) represents subtle sarcasm, as Michael Guinan says (*The Pentateuch*, 51). In Egyptian religion the sun god, after spending the night in the dark realm, defeats the darkness "just before dawn" and rises victorious to a new day. So it is at the very moment when Pharaoh (the sun god) should have been victorious that he and his armies are defeated by YHWH. It is YHWH alone who is God. The Egyptian god is powerless, and the Canaanite god, Sea, is only a weapon that YHWH uses to defeat the enemy.

The action of deliverance belongs entirely to YHWH, whether through the agency of Moses or not. Israel does nothing except to receive the divine favor. In this action, YHWH "creates" the people by giving them life where they had been facing certain death. Links to the creation narrative of Genesis 1 are abundant. Dry land appears as the sea withdraws (Gen. 1:9-10). The chaotic forces of the sea are subdued once and for all, and made an instrument in YHWH's hand. The people are "reborn" through the sea as from the birthing waters. A new history opens before them. From this moment on, they are YHWH's new people, just as Christians are made a new people by passing through the waters of baptism.

SECOND LESSON: ROMANS 9:1-5

These verses are the beginning of a crucial section of Romans, covering chapters 9–11. Our lectionaries contain only the opening passage and part of the conclusion in 11:13-16, 29-32 (next Sunday) and 11:33-36 (the Sunday following). It will be important to help the people make some sense of this truncated passage.

In chapters 9–11 of Romans, Paul addresses one of two major questions posed in chapter 3. The issue here is: If God is impartial, as Paul has been insisting, what about the promises to Israel? Is the price of insistence on divine impartiality that we must say that God is not faithful to God's promises? This is a crucial question for Gentile believers as well; after all, if God has been unfaithful to the promises to Israel, what assurance do the Gentiles have that God will not, sooner or later, be unfaithful to them also? The short answer is found at the beginning of chapter 11: "Has God rejected God's people? By no means!" Nevertheless, the solution is far from simple.

In this brief, personal introduction to chapter 9, Paul poses the question that opened chapter 3, "What advantage has the Jew?" by listing Israel's true privileges. The opening phrases are mysterious unless one has some knowledge of the context and the progress of the argument. It is his deep, familial concern for Israel that is causing Paul such anguish, even to the point that he wishes (in an expression that shows he is aware of the impossibility of what he is saying) that he could be "accursed and cut off from Christ" for their sake—something he has just shown to be unthinkable in 8:35-39. Paul here speaks as if Israel were under some kind of curse or imprisonment from which he would ransom them if (*per impossibile*) he could. Similarly, in Exod. 32:31-32 Moses expressed a willingness to sacrifice himself for the people.

In verse 4, Paul offers a list of seven advantages of the Israelites. (Whenever possible, in this argument, he refers to them, not by their political name, "Jews," but by the name given them by God, "Israel.") It is they who are God's adopted children (cf. Exod. 4:22; Deut. 14:1; Hos. 11:1). It is they who have enjoyed God's glorious presence in the tent of meeting and in the Temple—the reference is to God's *kābōd* or *shekinah,* (cf. Exod. 16:10; 40:34; 1 Kgs. 8:10-11). It was they who, in the persons of their ancestors, joined in covenants with God (the reference, in the plural, seems to be to the covenants with Noah, with Abraham, with Moses and the people in the wilderness, and with David), and it is they who received the law at Sinai. It is they who have presented YHWH with true worship. It is they who received the promises made to Abraham, Moses, Jacob (Israel) and David; the patriarchal ancestors are theirs.

Finally, the series of seven is capped by an eighth privilege, Israel's greatest glory by far: "From them, according to the flesh, comes the Messiah." There is great irony in the fact that, from Paul's point of view, it is precisely Israel's greatest title to glory that the people have failed to recognize for what it is.

The punctuation of the last part of verse 5 presents some difficulty. Two readings are almost equally probable: either ". . . Christ [or: the Messiah]. God who is over all be blessed for ever. Amen" as the RSV and NAB read; or "the Messiah [or: Christ], who is over all, God blessed forever. Amen" as in the NRSV. Because the earliest Greek manuscripts were not punctuated, either reading is possible. At present, the second punctuation, in which the title *theos* is applied to the Messiah/Christ, seems to be preferred, but because of the considerable weight of the alternative it should not be used as ammunition (as it was during the Arian controversies) in battles over the divinity of Christ. The first reading represents a Jewish formula of thanks and praise to God, and would be quite appropriate in this context.

The intent of these chapters is irenic; Paul is yearning and striving toward reconciliation. It is ironic, and it is certainly inappropriate in light of the events of the twentieth century, that they should be used to support and strengthen divisions between Christians and Jews, or even among Christians. It is important that our congregations understand that, according to Paul's logic, we are all God's children by adoption and, as the metaphor in the omitted section of chapter 11 so beautifully illustrates, it is the Gentiles who are the "wild olive shoots" grafted into the root of Israel, and not the other way around.

GOSPEL: MATTHEW 14:22-33

In Matthew's Gospel, the feeding of the multitude is followed immediately by the episode known as the "walking on water." Jesus sends the disciples ahead of him in a boat while he withdraws alone into the hills to pray. The disciples find themselves rowing against a strong headwind; late in the night, Jesus comes to them, walking on the sea. He calms the disciples' terror and, as soon as he enters the boat, the wind ceases. Into this story of a storm on the lake, as given in Mark, Matthew has inserted an incident that only he describes: Peter's request to approach Jesus on the water, his beginning to sink, his appeal to Jesus, and Jesus' admonition to him as "one of little faith."

The genre of the underlying story is that of an epiphany: Jesus does what God does, and the disciples behold him as a divine figure. In the literature of antiquity, only divine or quasi-divine beings can walk on water. There is thus an implicit claim made about Jesus' divinity. The disciples worship him, kneeling. This *proskynesis* is frequent in Matthew, beginning with the Magi falling down in worship before the child Jesus in 2:2, 11 and ending with the disciples' worshiping the risen Jesus in 28:17. Their confession of faith in v. 33: "Truly you are the Son of God!" partly anticipates Peter's more famous confession in Matt. 16:16.

In this story, Matthew continues the process of elevating the disciples in contrast to their treatment in Mark. In Mark's version, Jesus does not come directly to the aid of the disciples, but intends to pass them by; there is no episode featuring Peter; and at the end the disciples remain dumbfounded, not having found their way even to a "little faith." Matthew's version makes the disciples more insightful and gives prominence to Peter who, throughout this Gospel, remains the spokesperson for the disciples and the exemplary figure. Peter desires to imitate Jesus; he cries to Jesus in his distress; and he has faith, even if it is only "little." This characterization, *oligopistoi,* "people of little faith," is frequently applied to the disciples and is typical of them. They are not completely without faith, nor is their faith perfect. Even at the end, when they fall worshiping at the feet of the risen Jesus, "some doubted," just as Peter doubts in this instance ("You of little faith, why did you doubt?" v. 31). Still, they are not totally obstinate, like the disciples in Mark, nor blind like the Pharisees. Their faith is perfectible.

It is important to pay attention to the rich texture of scriptural allusions in this passage. In Canaanite myth and in the Old Testament, the chaos of the waters is regularly opposed to the power of the divine figure. YHWH of Israel is mighty in subduing the waves of death and the forces of the sea: see, for example, Pss. 77:19; Job 9:8; 38:16; Isa. 43:16; Sir. 24:5-6, and the great story of YHWH's power over the sea in Exodus 14. Jesus' words to the disciples: "Take heart, it is I; do not be afraid," echo the repeated reassurances in Isa. 41:13 and 43:1, 3. The very "it is I" is, in Greek, simply "I am," the name of God; in this context, it is an implicit claim on Jesus' own lips: cf. John 6:15-21; Mark 6:50.

(Clearly, this should not be regarded as a claim of the historical Jesus. The epiphany is understood retrospectively in light of Easter.) As Ulrich Luz has written, "Jesus here presents himself in the robe of a Hellenistic hero and speaking the language of the God of the Old Testament" (*Das Evangelium Matthäus {Mt 8–17}*, EKK 1/2 [Zürich, Braunschweig, and Neukirchen-Vluyn, 1990], 408).

The episode involving Peter is, as noted, important for Matthew's development of the character of Peter as the prominent figure among the twelve, but it may also depend on a pre-Matthean tradition, originating in a postresurrection appearance. If so, it may be reflected, in part, in John 21:7-8, another story involving Peter getting out of a boat to approach Jesus.

Many commentators see this pericope as a parable of the Matthean church under attack by the hostile forces symbolized by the wind. In that connection, it may be significant that, in Matthew, it is the boat that is said to be in distress, while in Mark it is the disciples themselves. The disciples are the leaders of the church. They are cast down because the church is threatened by recent events, but the Lord reaches out a hand to them. This is the attitude that should always characterize Christians as church: In time of trouble, the church turns to its Lord, crying, "Lord, save us!" and confessing, "Truly you are the Son of God!"

The story also reinforces the idea that to believe means to risk. Faith is not mere intellectual assent. It is the willingness to surrender ourselves to another, confident that our trust is not misplaced and that the other will sustain us. The presence of God does not dissipate the storm, for it is precisely in the midst of its dangers that the Christian experiences God's presence; it is when we are sinking that God lifts us up. In confident faith and trust we come closer to God and, even in the small measure of our faith, receive a share in the divine power that gives security in face of the forces of chaos.

Thirteenth Sunday after Pentecost

Lutheran	Roman Catholic	Episcopal	Common Lectionary
Isa. 56:1, 6-8	Isa. 56:1, 6-7	Isa. 56:1, 6-7	Exod. 16:2-15
Rom. 11:13-15, 29-32	Rom. 11:13-15, 29-32	Rom. 11:13-15, 29-32	Rom. 11:13-16, 29-32
Matt. 15:21-28	Matt. 15:21-28	Matt. 15:21-28	Matt. 15:21-28

FIRST LESSON: ISAIAH 56:1, 6-8

With chapter 56, we are at the beginning of the third section of the book of Isaiah, often called "Trito-Isaiah" or Third Isaiah. This is a collection of oracles apparently dating from the time after the people's return from the Babylonian exile. The first poem concerns temple worship for outsiders, and must therefore come from the period after the rebuilding of the Temple, ca. 515 B.C.E. That makes it one of the last additions to the book.

In contrast to Second Isaiah, there is a change in tone, vocabulary, and point of view, but especially in place: The setting is now Palestine. Because this is a collection of oracles, the mood can shift rapidly from disappointment to the anticipation of a glorious future. The outlook is at the same time more restrictive and more extended, for salvation is now envisioned, not for all Israel, but for a few, a "remnant," of the Jewish people, and at the same time is made available to Gentiles as well.

This is a period in which cultic worship was a preoccupation, at least for those who produced Israel's religious literature. We see this in the exilic and postexilic work of the Priestly writer(s), and also in Third Isaiah. "God's dwelling" is not thought of as embracing heaven and earth, as in Second Isaiah, but refers specifically to the Temple at Jerusalem; idolatry is not simply ridiculed, but is fiercely condemned. The spirituality of the book centers on temple, cultic worship, and the laws concerning the sabbath, fasting, and other regulations. Still, this section is not without ties to Second Isaiah; in fact, Third Isaiah introduces something new in biblical literature, in the form of quotations from and allusions to its predecessor (cf. 56:1 with 46:13). This suggests that the writer or writers may have been disciples of Second Isaiah who were anxious to preserve and extend their master's work.

A special theme of chapters 56–66 that appears immediately in this passage is the outreach to Gentiles, specifically proselytes to Israel's religion ("foreigners who join themselves to the Lord"). The poem opens with themes from Second Isaiah, but quickly focuses on matters of cultic worship. Verse 2, omitted in the lectionaries, is a beatitude reminiscent of Ps. 1:1; Jer. 17:7. The remainder of the reading concentrates on the status of "outsiders." In vv. 6-8 these are specifically foreigners, but the omitted verses concern those who were excluded from the cult for physical reasons, eunuchs in particular.

At this time, foreigners within Israel had certain limited rights and protections under the law. The effect of Third Isaiah's thinking is to extend those same rights to people outside the boundaries of the Land. This coordinates with the universalist ideas in such books as Ruth and Jonah. The poem functions like an entrance psalm (cf. Psalms 15 and 24, as well as Isa. 33:3-16 and 55:6-7), which admitted someone to the temple; hence the "foreigners" and "eunuchs" are officially welcomed into the Lord's dwelling. Those who formerly were excluded are now explicitly invited to enter the one place of encounter between YHWH and the chosen community.

Traditionally, eunuchs and other mutilated persons were refused admission to the *qahal YHWH*, the cultic assembly of Israel, just as mutilated animals were not to be offered in sacrifice (cf. Lev. 22:24; Deut. 23:1-9). In the case of eunuchs, the specific logic seems to have been that those deprived of the power to transmit life should not be associated with the creator of life; something similar could be said of the male animals for the offering. Persons born outside of sanctioned marriages were also excluded, because those born out of wedlock were outside the normal channels for the transmission of the covenant. Here, however, Third Isaiah specifically states that it is righteous conduct, in fact, the keeping of the covenant and the sabbath as the sign of covenant fidelity, that admit one to the community, and not birth or reproductive roles.

There were always some people in Israel who fell "outside" the usual prescriptions. Some young men were made eunuchs to work in the harems of the kings of Israel and Judah or those of foreign rulers. Some women did not marry or remained childless. The welcome into the community applies to all of them. This line of thinking continued as at least one strand of Israel's religious reflection down to the time of Jesus, for we find it in Wis. 3:13-14: "Blessed is the barren woman who is undefiled. . . . Blessed also is the eunuch whose hands have done no lawless deed." Third Isaiah promises these people "a monument and a name better than sons and daughters" (v. 5); in other words, a continuing presence within the life of Israel surpassing that gained in the normal way by producing children.

In our time we are not in the business of producing eunuchs either for employment in harems or for their singing voices. However, there are a great many people who have been made to feel "outsiders" to the Christian community because of their physical state (Are our churches accessible to the handicapped? Are they truly welcome among us? Are the childless made to feel at home? Does the language we use in worship tell women that they are excluded?) or because they have sexual orientations or lifestyles that are "outside" what has been considered the "mainstream" of Christian life. Third Isaiah's poem is a rebuke against exclusivism. This reading offers a prime opportunity for the preacher to extend welcome and inclusion to those so often excluded, "for my house shall be called a house of prayer for all peoples" (Cf. Mark 11:17 and parallels).

ALTERNATIVE FIRST LESSON: EXODUS 16:2-15

This account of the gift of manna (and/or quails) is part of the semicontinuous reading. It relates to the Gospel reading only incidentally because of the theme of God's gift of bread to God's people.

The passage is a composition mainly of the Priestly writer (with possible influences from the Elohist), but contains some Yahwist sections as well. The Priestly and Elohist passages (16:2-3, 6-13) are distinguished by the motif of the people's "murmuring" or "complaining," in this case because they are hungry. (In the immediately preceding pericope, 15:22-27, they had complained because they were thirsty, and YHWH had given them potable water.) In the Yahwist sections (16:4-5, 14-15), on the other hand, the initiative comes directly from YHWH. As far as the Yahwist is concerned, what is given at this point is manna; the quails come later (cf. Numbers 11). The Priestly and Elohist writers refer to the gift of "flesh to eat," that is, quails, at this point (cf. verse 13a). Finally, there are a few notes from the Deuteronomist, especially at the end of verse 16. These introduce the theme of God's "testing" the people.

Psalm 78:17-31 has a different outlook on this episode. In that version, the quails turn out to be poisonous, the vehicle of divine vengeance on the people for having "tested" God.

In purely scientific terms, the "manna" is a regularly occurring phenomenon of the Sinai desert, the droppings of scale insects that infest the tamarisk bushes in that region. It is sweet and full of carbohydrates, but contains no protein and does not keep well, hence the need to gather it daily. Contemporary Arabs still call it "mann." The "quails" are *coturnix coturnix,* small birds that visit the region in flocks in March and April.

It is particularly clear that this passage operates on two levels and reflects the metaphoric character of the people's journey. A crisis over *food* results in a crisis of *faith.* Wavering belief in God's ability to care for the people's ordinary needs leads to a lack of faith in God's ability to act in extraordinary ways, that is, to be God for Israel (see Terence E. Fretheim, *Exodus* [Louisville: Westminster/John Knox, 1991], 181–87).

The very naturalness of the phenomena is of the essence. It is not only (or even often) that God acts in extraordinary ways. Like the "sound of silence" that Elijah heard, God's good purpose and gifts to humanity are in all that surrounds us every day—if we have not corrupted them. The very rhythm of our days and of the week is part of God's plan for creation—at least so the sacred authors believed. When we "trash" the earth that is meant to provide for us, when we destroy our own lives and those of others by frantically working and hoarding, so that there is not enough to go around, we are as rebellious as Israel in the wilderness, and just as surely headed for trouble.

SECOND LESSON: ROMANS 11:13-15(16), 29-32

This truncated reading, together with verses 33-36 which are read next Sunday, concludes Paul's reflection on the fulfillment of the promises to Israel in Romans 9–11. Fortuitously, it deals with the theme of the Gentiles and their relationship to Israel, thus coordinating with the first and Gospel readings, a fortunate coincidence of which the preacher may wish to take advantage.

Like the first reading from Third Isaiah, this passage is addressed to the Gentiles, the "outsiders," but in this case the Gentiles are inclined to see themselves as the "insiders," and Paul is admonishing them not to think themselves better than the Jews; on the contrary. Paul's very purpose in becoming an "apostle to the Gentiles" (an epithet he applies to himself here and in Gal. 2:7-8) is to stimulate his own Jewish people to jealousy and thus to save as many of them as possible. Paul still thinks of himself as a Jew, and he calls the Jewish people, literally, "my flesh."

There are some difficult phrases in v. 15. "Their rejection" refers *not* to God's rejecting God's people (which is impossible), but to the majority of those people having rejected the gospel. "The reconciliation of the world" hints at a sweeping universalism in Paul's thought (cf. 2 Cor. 5:19, which speaks of "God's reconciling *the world* to Godself). The (temporary) rejection of the gospel on the part of some of the Jews has made possible an extension of God's reconciliation to Gentiles and perhaps to the entire universe; in a reverse movement, the acceptance of the gospel by the Gentiles will lead to the reconciliation of the remaining Jews, and thus the complete fulfillment of God's will to reconcile the whole world in Christ. "Life from the dead" is unclear; it may refer to the general resurrection, to the benefit received by the Gentiles, or (very probably) to the passage of the Jewish people themselves from death to life.

In v. 16, Paul employs two figures: the dough and the root. The former refers to the "first fruits" of the grain harvest, the "wave offering" (cf. Num. 15:18-21; Jer. 11:16-17). Thus the "remnant" of Israel already converted gives assurance that the whole mass is sanctified. The latter, the "root," seems to refer to the ancestors of Israel, through whom salvation has come into the world. A reflection could be offered here on the paired concepts (dough and root), which are similar to the paired parables of mustard seed and leaven in Matt. 13:31-33 (see the commentary for the Tenth Sunday after Pentecost). This pair calls to mind the traditional activities of women and of men. God sanctifies the dough and the plant; God hallows women and men; God is intimate with, God *is* all that we commonly identify as "feminine" and "masculine."

An important point to be emphasized, especially because it is underscored by the metaphor of the olive tree that is omitted from the reading, is that, both now and in the eschatological future, the Gentiles receive their share in God's salvation *through Israel*—in the present, this is a result of Israel's fall and its rejection of the gospel; in the future, the Gentiles will continue to share in that salvation as a consequence of Israel's restoration to its "full number." In other words, God's promise always has been and always will be extended to the world through Israel; it comes to the Gentiles through Jesus Christ as the representative of Israel. Therefore the Gentiles have nothing to boast of and no reason to be hostile toward or to feel superior to the people of Israel.

The omission of v. 28 from the reading destroys the logical symmetry of the concluding argument, which is a chiastic construction. Verse 29 follows on v. 28: The Jews remain God's beloved because God's gifts and God's call are irrevocable. The "disobedience" that is the theme of vv. 30-32 is equivalent to disbelief. We see again that Paul's view of the Gentiles agrees with that of his Jewish kin: In not recognizing the presence of God in Israel, in failing to believe, they were "disobedient." Now Jewish disobedience (i.e., their disbelief in Jesus as the Messiah of Israel) has opened the way to the display of God's mercy toward the Gentiles; so in the future the mercy shown to the Gentiles will be extended also to the Jewish people. Ultimately, all humankind, whether Jews or Gentiles, have been unfaithful, disbelieving, disobedient, but God makes use of their very sinfulness to manifest God's bounty, God's mercy—to reveal who God really is.

GOSPEL: MATTHEW 15:21-28

This is one of those rare occasions in which a woman appears as the heroine of the Sunday Gospel—for this really is the woman's story. It will be important to see, and to point out, the importance of her character and her actions, while noting the ways in which Matthew has altered Mark's version of the story to suit the purposes of his own community.

The story of the woman in chapter 15 parallels, in Matthew's version, the story of the centurion in 8:5-13. These are the only two healings in Matthew's Gospel that are done on behalf of Gentiles, and they follow a similar pattern. In neither case does Jesus go to the home of the Gentile, and the parallels (as well as the Markan version) have led many commentators to assume that the healing of the woman's daughter takes place at a distance, like the healing of the centurion's servant. This is not entirely clear from Matthew's text, however, and the statement in v. 28 that the girl was healed "instantly" makes it possible, and even likely, that Matthew envisions the daughter as being present along with her mother.

The woman is doubly or even trebly marginal: She is, apparently, a woman alone, for she has no male relative to speak for her. (It is interesting to observe that, in Matthew's Gospel in general, women who approach Jesus are not identified in relational terms as "daughter of," or "wife of." This probably reflects something important about relationships within the Christian community, the new family of God.) She seems to travel outside her own country to find help for her daughter (although exegetes disagree about whether the encounter takes place in or near the city or in one of the nearby Jewish villages). She is a Gentile, and therefore unclean. In Mark's version, she is "a Greek, a Syrophoenician by birth," thus very possibly one of the "upper crust" in the Greek cities of Tyre and Sidon; Matthew makes her "a Canaanite," hence a representative of the original inhabitants of the land of Israel and one of Israel's antagonists. By meeting Jesus on his own terms and possibly in his own country, and by the honorific titles she bestows on him, the woman in Matthew's story acknowledges Jesus' priority in the divine plan of salvation. The message for Matthew's church is that the Gentiles, too, are worthy of Jesus' (i.e., the Christian community's) attention, and that ultimately (although not at first) the gospel is to be extended to them as well. This responds to the apparent sharp conflicts within Matthean Christianity about the possibility of converting Gentiles and the order of priorities.

In addition to being a woman and a Gentile, our heroine comes seeking aid for a daughter. Daughters were an expendable commodity in the ancient world, a drug on the market. Few families raised more than one, because they were expensive to dower and therefore a liability rather than an asset to their family of birth. If a daughter were to die young, well, she was no great loss at best; if she were possessed by a demon, as in this case, she might—under the right circumstances—be turned into an asset, like the slave girl Paul meets in Acts 16:16-18, whose owners were miffed at the loss of her powers of divination and therefore of their income. To go out of one's way to obtain a daughter's *release* from a demon was certainly above and beyond necessity. This woman comes screaming to Jesus, and she goes on shouting despite the disciples' attempts to shut her up or get rid of her.

Matthew, even more than Mark, depicts Jesus as turning a cold shoulder to the woman and addressing her in hostile terms. His saying about his being sent to "the lost sheep of the house of Israel" confirms and underscores the disciples' rejection of the woman's plea by giving that rejection a salvation-historical basis. We should not gloss over or explain away this attitude on the part of Jesus. It can be an important occasion for emphasizing Jesus' humanity and his genuine involvement with and identification with his Jewish people, with all their prejudices and ingrained attitudes—much like those Paul expresses in his letter to the Romans. For Matthew's community, this portrait of Jesus underscores the same point that Paul is making in Romans 9–11, namely that God had remained faithful to the promises to Israel, and that the post-Easter missionary command in 28:18-20 represented a fundamental alteration in God's plan for the salvation of the whole world.

Under the circumstances, it takes extraordinary courage on the part of the woman to renew her plea for help. Ultimately, it is her persistence that pays off, and she is the only person in any of the four Gospels who ever gets the better of Jesus in an argument. This is especially clear in Mark, while Matthew has expanded the dialogue in such a way as to portray the woman as an example of faith. She addresses Jesus with titles that emphasize his dignity and recall his genealogy; these words associate her with the Jewish crowds in Matt. 21:9, 15, and distinguish her from the leaders who refused Jesus the titles that were rightfully his. Matthew makes Jesus' hostility toward her even sharper than in Mark by omitting the observation, "Let the children be fed first" (Mark 7:27). The background situation itself reflects economic tensions between the Greek cities and the Jewish countryside, which had to hand over its produce to fulfill its tax obligation to the cities, whether or not there was enough bread left for "the children," that is, the Jewish people. The reference to Gentiles as "dogs" was not uncommon, but it was no less an insult when offered directly to the woman's face.

Nevertheless, she is not deterred. Her reply turns Jesus' remark back on him, but in a respectful way; she acknowledges the priority of Israel, even obliquely calls them "masters," but without withdrawing her claim and her appeal. Jesus, vanquished, praises her: "Woman, great is your faith!" Thus the portrait of the woman as an example of humble yet insistent faith is completed. We note that she is the only person in Matthew's Gospel who is said to have "great faith." In fact, the typical characterization of the disciples is "people of little faith," as appeared, for example, in the previous story about the disciples in the boat. The faith of the Gentiles may be, then, a shame and a spur to the Jewish disciples. The woman, because of her faith, receives what she desires: "Her daughter was healed instantly."

One might say that the faith and persistence of this woman are not unknown to Christian women, from that day to this. If they fail to receive what they are seeking, in church and society—the healing of their daughters, the restoration of themselves and their sisters to the dignity Jesus accorded them—whose fault is it, and whose example is being followed?

Fourteenth Sunday after Pentecost

Lutheran	Roman Catholic	Episcopal	Common Lectionary
Exod. 6:2-8	Isa. 22:19-23	Isa. 51:1-6	Exod. 17:1-7
Rom. 11:33-36	Rom. 11:33-36	Rom. 11:33-36	Rom. 11:33-36
Matt. 16:13-20	Matt. 16:13-20	Matt. 16:13-20	Matt. 16:13-20

FIRST LESSON: EXODUS 6:2-8

This narrative, from the Priestly source, is that author's version of the divine self-revelation and the commissioning of Moses that had been recounted from the Elohist and Yahwist sources in Exodus 3–4. In its present context, therefore, it represents a second version of the same events. In this version of the story, Moses and Aaron have already approached Pharaoh with the demand that the people be allowed to go into the desert to sacrifice and have been refused; moreover, in retaliation the people's tasks have been made more severe, and the people's representatives have accused Moses and Aaron of making life worse for them than it already was, a complaint that Moses passes on to God. For the Priestly writer, what follows is the necessary next step in the covenantal history that began with Noah and Abraham.

The God who made a covenant with the patriarchs was known to them by the name "El Shaddai" (cf. Gen. 17:1; 35:11-12; 48:3-4). According to the Priestly source, and in contradiction to the position of the Yahwist (cf. Gen. 13:4), the divine name YHWH was reserved for the generation that would enter the covenant at Sinai and follow its precepts. The disclosure of the divine name at this point is evidence that the time has come for this sacred relationship to be solemnized. Previously, God did not reveal God's own name to the patriarchs, even when extending to them the promise that is now to be fulfilled. Now the "fullness of time" has come, and the divine name is made known.

"El Shaddai" has traditionally been translated into English as "God Almighty." It may be understood, on the basis of its root meaning and some early texts from the Ancient Near East, to mean "the god of the mountain." The gods who met in council on the mountain (much like the Olympian gods of Greece) were the "Shaddayim." "El (= god) Shaddai" might be the presiding deity of this divine council, like Zeus Olympios. We need also to note that the words for "mountain" and for the female breast are the same in their root. Hence, in calling their God by this name, the earlier generations of Israelites may have been indicating their understanding of their God as both paternal and maternal. See Gen. 49:25, the blessing of Joseph by

> . . . the Almighty [El Shaddai] who will bless you
> with blessings of heaven above,
> blessings of the deep that lies beneath,
> blessings *of the breasts and of the womb.*

God's self-naming is not merely that, but also an assertion of power and authority, not only in the present, but in the past as well. Linking the deeds now to be accomplished with God's past promises shows that this is one and the same God. Note, in particular, the emphasis on the land of promise. The covenant between God and God's people is fundamentally identified with the promise of the land, for it is only when they are dwelling in that land, no longer as "sojourners," but as permanent possessors, that the people will be able to live according to the covenant they are about to undertake.

The commissioning of Moses begins with verse 5 and extends beyond the end of the reading. Moses is sent first to the Israelites (vv. 6-8), and then to Pharaoh (v. 10). The statement "I am YHWH" is repeated three times within this passage, because for the Priestly writer one of the primary reasons for YHWH's mighty acts in history is to make God's name known and God's power recognized and acknowledged by all people, but first and foremost by God's own people, Israel.

In connection with the Gospel for today, this reading emphasizes the theophany aspect of the Gospel: the revelation of Jesus as Messiah and Son of God. It makes clear, in a way that the alternative readings do not (or do less clearly), that the ultimate purpose of Moses' commissioning, and later of Peter's commissioning, is the creation of a people and the revelation of God's sovereignty in a special place: within the community that is God's own, that acknowledges God to be God.

ALTERNATIVE FIRST LESSON: ISAIAH 22:19-23

The Roman Catholic lectionary calls for this passage as the first reading of the Sunday because of the linking word "key" in the Gospel. Just as Eliakim is to be made steward and given "the key of the house of David," so Peter will be given "the keys of the kingdom of heaven" (Matt. 16:19).

Verse 19 is actually the end of the preceding oracle, directed against Shebna, "master of the palace." With v. 20 begins a new oracle, signaled by the words "on that day." It looks forward to a messianic age, and so operates on both a historical and a metahistorical plane. Eliakim will be put in Shebna's place and will be closely associated with the royal house of Hezekiah. For his becoming a "father" to the inhabitants of Jerusalem and the house of Judah, see Isa. 9:6, as well as Gen. 45:8 (Joseph as "a father" to Pharaoh when steward of Pharaoh's possessions); Job 29:16 (Job "a father to the needy"); and Judg. 5:7 (Deborah "a mother in Israel"). The "key of the house of David" symbolizes Eliakim's authority over all those dwelling in the royal palace and his control over all the government offices, while its being placed "on his shoulder" may reflect the rite of his investiture. Verse 23 indicates that Eliakim's family will participate in his prerogatives during his lifetime, and may inherit his office or, at least, enjoy the honor that accrues to the family as the result of his having held it.

Unfortunately, v. 25 indicates that Eliakim did not measure up: He "will be cut down and fall." In contrast to King Hezekiah, whose prayers gain him personal redemption (although he is not able to save the people), the rest of the people suffer fates corresponding to their faith or lack thereof. The whole oracle illustrates God's continuing awareness of and response to the obedience or disobedience of individuals, even in a time of national judgment.

The Gospel reading tells of the bestowal of the "power of the keys" on Peter as the leading disciple, clearly the most important of the Twelve as far as Matthew's community was concerned. (The firm fixing of the tent peg could also be interpreted in connection with Peter's nickname.) Reflecting another line of interpretation in the early church, Rev. 3:7 applies this passage directly to "the holy one." It is the exalted Lord in person who holds the key to the heavenly realm.

ALTERNATIVE FIRST LESSON: ISAIAH 51:1-6

This reading from Isaiah is tied to the Gospel reading by another key word: "rock." The oracle, near the end of Second Isaiah, is spoken as a consolation to the people (and to their prophet) in a situation of return from exile that was far from the golden ideal they had imagined. Though permitted to return to Jerusalem, the exiles were restricted to a tiny enclave (twenty by twenty-five miles) that was insufficient to support them. Like the generation in the wilderness, they cried out in despair and anguish. Still worse for the prophet, he found himself unable to win over the majority of people to his point of view, nor could he prevail over rival and controlling religious groups, such as the Priestly school and those who coalesced around Ezekiel.

But despite all these problems, the oracle gives assurance of YHWH's consoling presence in the holy city. YHWH will "comfort" Zion and will make her a fruitful mother; the language is the same as that of 2 Sam. 12:24, when David "comforted" Bathsheba after the death of their child. The people are urged to be conscious of their roots: of the rock from which they were hewn (a favorite metaphor, cf. Deut. 32:4, 18), of their prototypical ancestors, Abraham and Sarah. This is the only reference to Sarah's name in the Old Testament outside the book of Genesis. The word "quarry" in Hebrew sounds like the word "woman," and may suggest carrying the metaphor further. The once-barren womb of Sarah was the rock, the "quarry" from which God raised up a nation. When God called Abraham, Abraham was "one," not in the sense of being a man alone, but (in the meaning of the Hebrew) as a man who was "one with" his wife Sarah, without whom he would have been a barren rock indeed.

The returning people themselves are living proof that YHWH is a keeper of promises (vv. 1-3). Eden, once a golden image of the past, is now a symbol of Israel's future. The remaining three verses draw on First Isaiah (cf. 2:3) and on the major servant songs in Second Isaiah (42:1; 49:6; 53:1; 42:4). The language of the servant songs is here clearly applied to Israel as a whole. There is also allusion to the songs of Zion, such as Psalms 46 and 48. The whole composition is placed within the context of the joyful ascent of Mount Zion. The "arm of the Lord" represents deliverance (as in Exodus) as well as creation itself (cf. Jer. 27:5) and the overcoming of the original chaos. As in the Priestly writer's description of creation in Genesis 1, so here in Second Isaiah the reigning deities of the nations, the sun, stars, and moon (summarized in v. 6 as "the heavens") are dismissed as ephemeral nothings that will "vanish like smoke," while God's salvation endures forever.

ALTERNATIVE FIRST LESSON: EXODUS 17:1-7

In this section of the Exodus narrative, the people of Israel "test" God for a third time, after previous complaints about the lack of potable water and then about having no food. Here again, water is the issue: This time they have no water at all. The people do not believe that God can provide for their needs, can be their God in the wilderness. In a certain sense, they have logic on their side: If it is true that only when dwelling in "the land that has been given to them for their own possession" they can fully be God's people, then perhaps this God is (like most gods) a local divinity whose power does not extend to the desert through which they are traveling. Maybe they need a god for the journey, and another god for the land.

God is apparently not perturbed by the people's murmuring—unlike Moses, who scolds them and appeals in exasperation to God for help. God simply orders Moses to strike the rock with the same miraculous rod that formerly struck the Nile (with the reverse effect: At that time the Egyptian people's drinking water was made unfit for use). The elders are taken along as witnesses, and when Moses does as God has ordered, water springs forth from the rock. The people's expectation is proved wrong: God is in charge of this hostile environment as well as of the promised land.

Most people are more familiar with the duplicate or parallel narrative in Num. 20:1-13, in which the story of Moses' drawing water from the rock is used to explain why Moses and Aaron did not enter the promised land. That motif is not in view here. In this version, the only issue is a demonstration of God's power, which is independent of and far beyond human expectations.

Because this is a semicontinuous narrative, the "rock" association in this passage is only coincidental. It is not intended to harmonize with the Gospel reading.

SECOND LESSON: ROMANS 11:33-36

With this noble hymn, Paul concludes the section of his letter to the Romans dealing with the problem of Israel's unbelief. The ultimate judgment belongs to God, and God's judgment is also God's mercy: Both are far beyond human comprehension, unsearchable, inscrutable. The three exclamations in v. 33 are balanced by three rhetorical questions in inverse order, drawn from the Old Testament. Verse 34 is quoted almost verbatim from the Septuagint Greek of Isa. 40:13, while v. 35 corresponds to the Targum (Aramaic verse-by-verse commentary) on Job 15:8. The final couplet is at the same time a lovely biblical doxology and a reflection of the best of Hellenistic philosophical thought; many decades later, the same idea would be found in the writings of the late Stoic philosopher-emperor, Marcus Aurelius.

This may be an early Christian hymn that Paul has adapted to his own purposes. In its present location it emphasizes, with the help of the verse from Isaiah, that God is no one's debtor; no one can claim salvation as a matter of right, whether that person be Gentile or Jew. Thus, in the end, the solution to Paul's dilemma lies not with Paul nor with any other human agent, but with God.

The final verse, with its beautiful summary of the best of Christian and pagan thinking, is a fine expression of creation spirituality and makes an excellent starting point for a reflection on the unity of creation.

GOSPEL: MATTHEW 16:13-20

The scene at Caesarea Philippi is so familiar to Christian believers, and has borne so much polemical freight over the centuries, that it presents a great challenge to preachers. The observations presented here are intended to provide springboards for further reflection.

Jesus' question to his followers regarding popular perceptions of his identity is found in all the Gospels in some form (cf. Mark 8:27; Luke 9:18; John 6:66-69). It would hardly be surprising, within a culture of fixed roles and statuses, that one person would ask another, or a group of others, to aid in self-definition, because in such a culture it *is* others, from the close kinship group to the larger society, who define who one is. For us, of course, in post-Easter hindsight, it is a given that Jesus knew who he was, but that need not be the immediate message of the question and response.

Matthew adopts the question, "Who do people say that I am?" from Mark's account, but replaces the personal pronoun with the phrase "Son of Man," or "Son of humanity," which bears a load of associations, both with other such references within this Gospel and with the "figure like a son of man" in Daniel 7. Clearly, though, it is not a messianic title at this point, because that would make the question pointless or make Jesus sound like a modern dictator seeking sycophantic praise and affirmation. Matthew inserts Jeremiah into the list of possible identities; he is the only evangelist who mentions Jeremiah (cf. 2:17; 27:9). The fact that in the other two passages Jeremiah consistently appears as a prophet of doom suggests that here it is only one more false identification. There are also allusions to Jeremiah elsewhere in the Gospel, especially in Jesus' discourse in the Temple.

Peter's response to the second question, regarding the disciples' own identification of Jesus, represents the first time that a disciple affirms Jesus' messiahship. The expansion of Mark's simple "You are the Messiah" with the phrase "the son of the living God" defuses whatever hostility might be connected with political and military notions of the Messiah's role. More than this, the confession Peter speaks is complete (contrast Mark's version). It is the christological confession of the Matthean community. But despite the praise of Peter that follows, we already know (from 11:25-27) that his knowledge is a gift from God.

The following three verses (17-19) are unique to Matthew, and they contain some language that is found only in Matthew's Gospel, especially the reference to the "church" (in the four Gospels, only here and at Matt. 18:17), and the notion of the "keys of the kingdom" that parallels Peter with the royal steward in Isa. 22:22. Matthew is always careful to distinguish "church" (the Jesus community) from "synagogue." In parallel, as holder of the "keys," Peter is clearly meant to open the realm of heaven to believers, in contrast to the scribes and Pharisees who, according to 23:13, lock people out of it. The play on Peter's name, which in Greek and even more in Aramaic is almost the same as the word for "rock," may reflect an actual nickname for Simon, in line with his "rocky" personality. The nickname probably goes back to Simon's actual lifetime among the disciples. Its meaning is not as clear as at first appears, because *kepha/petros* refers to a smallish stone, such as one might throw, rather than the bedrock of "upon this rock." One good suggestion is that the original nickname for Simon, the first called, made him something like the "jewel" of the community, a "stone" in the sense of "precious stone." Matthew's story then links the well-known nickname with a particular incident.

What is the origin of this story? At least three possibilities have been suggested: an incident during the historical life of Jesus, a postresurrection appearance story, or a foundation story regarding the post-Easter leadership of the church. It has been argued that the language of these verses is sufficiently Semitic to make an origin during Jesus' lifetime possible, but few exegetes hold that position now. The fact that the macarism and etiological legend concerning Peter's name, together with the sayings about the keys and binding or loosing, are found only in Matthew's Gospel makes it more likely that these traditions are peculiar to Matthew's church and date from some time after the Easter events.

If this is a foundation story belonging to a Matthean community, one likely location for it is Antioch—traditionally, although not universally, regarded as the place where this Gospel was written. Antioch was a focal point for the controversy over Jewish versus Gentile church membership and requirements for participation. The extremes on this question were represented by James, the Jerusalem leader, and Paul, the "apostle to the Gentiles," for whom Antioch was a missionary base. Peter, also associated with Antioch, stood somewhere in between. We note that the Gospel of Thomas, Logion 12, assigns the key role among the disciples to James. On the other hand, "flesh and blood has not revealed this to you" could be an oblique riposte to Paul (see Gal. 1:15-16). In a struggle over leadership in the Antioch community, the followers of Peter may have stood in a middle position, an ideal compromise validated by this story.

If this is the case, it is, to say the least, ironic that an "ecumenical" story designed to facilitate compromise over leadership roles should have become the focus of so much interchurch controversy over the papacy and authority. It will be well if, as a vehicle for preaching, it can be restored to its irenic and ecumenical role. Although the power to bind and loose is assigned to Peter in this story, in Matt. 18:18 it is extended to the whole church. This double emphasis in Matthew should be noted. Peter's "primacy" consists in being the tradent and guarantor of the teaching of Jesus, the church's greatest treasure.

Fifteenth Sunday after Pentecost

Lutheran	Roman Catholic	Episcopal	Common Lectionary
Jer. 15:15-21	Jer. 20:7-9	Jer. 15:15-21	Exod. 19:1-9
Rom. 12:1-8	Rom. 12:1-2	Rom. 12:1-8	Rom. 12:1-13
Matt. 16:21-26	Matt. 16:21-27	Matt. 16:21-27	Matt. 16:21-28

FIRST LESSON: JEREMIAH 15:15-21; 20:7-9

This reading and the alternate from the Roman Catholic lectionary form parts of two of Jeremiah's "confessions." Their literary pattern is similar to that of psalms of lament.

Historically, these poems probably date from one of the lowest points of Jeremiah's life, during the reign of King Jehoiakim. At this time, in the late seventh century B.C.E., Assyria was in collapse and Babylon was in the ascendant, but had not yet wrested power over Palestine from the hands of Egypt. King Josiah of Judah had taken advantage of Assyria's instability to launch a political and religious reform that even extended to the northern kingdom, but his efforts collapsed with his death at Megiddo, and the Egyptian pharaoh, Neco, deposed his successor and replaced him with Jehoiakim (609–598). Under Jehoiakim religious syncretism was revived. Jeremiah, who had approved of Josiah's reforms, now sees his hopes dashed as Israel once again abandons its allegiance to YHWH.

Thematically, the poem in 15:15-21 repeats elements from Jeremiah's call (cf. 1:9). It is, in a sense, a second appeal to the prophet to resume his prophetic role. The prophet's complaint (vv. 15-18) is met by a response from YHWH (vv. 19-21), but Jeremiah's situation is a terrible one, caught as he is between an insistent God and a hostile people.

Jeremiah speaks angrily and accusingly to God, even comparing God's fidelity to that of the brooks of Palestine, most of which dry up in the summer. Both here and in Job 6:16-21, those streams symbolize the deepest form of deception. This is the language of someone who is on intimate terms with God, who can say what she or he really feels. Jeremiah expects YHWH to make good on previous commitments: "you know; remember"! And yet YHWH has proved as unreliable and deceitful as a desert brook! In fact, Jeremiah has been more faithful than YHWH: Jeremiah preached unpalatable news, and it is no wonder he is outcast and in trouble. Nevertheless, why did YHWH not stand by him?

YHWH's response is not the consoling message we usually expect after a lament; instead, it is a confirmation of Jeremiah's mission, repeating the terms of his first call (cf. 1:18-19), but in harsh tones. YHWH does not even offer a defense. Instead of an assurance, there is a condition imposed; the prophetic call is not a simple gift. Jeremiah will be restored only if he converts ("if you return"). He must reject rebellious thoughts and again speak the words of YHWH to the people ("what is precious and not what is worthless"). The implication is that Jeremiah has not been as faithful as he claims, or else that he must be still more faithful than he has been.

We should notice that, in these poems, it is Jeremiah's very expression of anger that is the proof of his fidelity to YHWH. If he were resigned, if he simply gave up his allegiance, he would not be so distressed. It is precisely the most faithful believers who seethe with anger when they see the very institutions that are intended to serve and promote God's good will being turned to perverted purposes. There is, in our churches, far too little outlet for the justified rage of the downtrodden. Jeremiah can be a model for those who speak the truth but find their words rejected by religious as well as civil authorities, for those whose outcry when they are beaten and abused falls on deaf ears—for all those who, because they suffer at the hands of those who are supposed to represent God, are made to wonder whether God has abandoned and betrayed them. The message of the text is that God is faithful and will vindicate those who remain faithful to God, but it does not say when, nor does it diminish the price they have to pay at the hands of their oppressors.

In Jer. 20:7-9 we reach the climax of the whole crisis: Despairing, Jeremiah accuses YHWH of having forsaken him, and even of having deceived him. This lament is located by the editor of the book immediately after an incident in which Jeremiah was arrested and put into the stocks by the priest Pashhur. It appears as Jeremiah's response to that event. The verb *pātâ* means first of all "to seduce" and is applied to the seduction of a virgin by a man (cf. Exod. 22:15). In its extended meaning, "deceive," it is sometimes applied to false prophets being tricked by YHWH (cf. 1 Kgs. 22:19-23; Ezek. 14:9). All the more reason for Jeremiah to be outraged, for he is no false prophet, and yet he feels himself tricked, seduced, and abandoned!

The other verb in v. 7, translated "you have overpowered me," or "you were too strong for me," is *ḥāzaq*, "to seize." It also figures in narratives of sexual seduction (e.g., Deut. 22:25; 2 Sam. 13:12, 14; Prov. 7:13). God's treatment of Jeremiah has been both seductive and irresistible; as the rest of the text points out, the urge to prophesy was so strong that he could not hold back, no matter what the consequences. Part of the deception, it seems, is that although YHWH promised Jeremiah that he would speak both good and bad to the people (1:10, "to pluck up and to pull down, to destroy and to overthrow, to build and to plant"), the prophet has never been able to preach anything but disaster, which is why he has been persecuted, while other prophets are speaking peace (even though there is no peace).

FIFTEENTH SUNDAY AFTER PENTECOST

In this selection, no exit from Jeremiah's dilemma is offered. He prophesies because he must, but the result for him is only trouble. As Walter Brueggemann writes, "The prophet has only two alternatives, and neither one works. When he speaks, Yahweh does not support him. When he is silent, Yahweh does not console him" (*A Commentary on the Book of Jeremiah 1–25: To Pluck Up, To Tear Down* [Grand Rapids: Wm. B. Eerdmanns, 1988], 174). The prophet's terrible situation could only be endured with YHWH's sustaining help, and this is withheld. The selected passage leaves Jeremiah where he is, with no solution.

ALTERNATIVE FIRST LESSON: EXODUS 19:1-9

In the twelve-stage procession from Egypt to the promised land (as the scheme of things is conceived by the Priestly writer), the Israelites have reached stage seven: YHWH's mountain, Sinai. The passage designated for the reading is composed partly of Priestly material (vv. 1-2a), partly of Yahwist writing (only v. 2b in this selection), and partly of Elohist material (vv. 3a and 9). The liturgical poem in vv. 3b-8 comes from a special source that may have been incorporated in the Elohist writing.

This is "the third new moon" since the departure from Egypt: The first was the beginning of spring, Passover, and this third one corresponds to what was in the later Jewish calendar the Feast of Weeks, or Pentecost. There is some evidence that as early as the second century B.C.E. some Jewish groups connected Pentecost with the giving of the law at Sinai, but it cannot be shown that this was generally accepted in Judaism until the third century C.E. Israel encamps at the foot of the mountain—the same mountain where Moses first encountered God in Exodus 3—and Moses goes up the mountain to meet God again. It is first said that Moses goes up "to *ʾĕlōhîm,*" (the Elohist's name for God), but in the subsequent text the name YHWH reappears: and YHWH called to him out of "the mountain." We are to understand that YHWH lives in "the heavens," and is not a local deity of the mountain; YHWH descends on the mountain to meet Moses, who ascends the mountain in an opposite movement.

Verses 4-8 have been called a "covenant in miniature." The word "covenant" appears only once, but the formal elements are all there, including a recital of God's historic deeds on behalf of Israel, the requirements of the covenant: "Obey my voice and keep my covenant," and the reward for compliance: "You shall be my treasured possession out of all the peoples." The "treasured possession" is *sĕgullâ* (cf. Deut. 7:6; 14:2; 26:18; Pss. 135:4), a term used to describe the finest treasures of the wealthy and of kings; in Near Eastern literature we sometimes read that a ruler is the god's *sĕgullâ*. In this passage, however, we find that it is the whole people of Israel that is YHWH's chosen treasure. YHWH has brought the people into the wilderness (cf. Hos. 2:14), has borne them up as tenderly as an eagle carries her young (v. 4; cf. Deut. 32:10-12 for the extended image of

43

God as a mother eagle) to join with them in a covenant and to make them God's very own people, a precious possession.

There is a steady reciprocal movement throughout the passage. At Sinai, YHWH had seen the suffering of the people and resolved to act (Exod. 3:7-8); now at Sinai the people, having seen YHWH's works (v. 4) are called upon to act. Obedience to God's commandments is the consequence of a relationship already established by God's initiative on their behalf. Will they agree to be YHWH's people by obeying YHWH's will and building their God a dwelling in their midst? Will they consent to be a "priestly kingdom and a holy nation"? They are to be a "priestly kingdom" because only they, among all the nations, can offer true worship; they are set apart and sacred among the nations as priests are among the people. This also means that they are to live and act on behalf of the earth, God's creation and possession. They are a servant nation, God's mediator to the world and the nations. The notion of a priestly people strikes a blow against clericalism and hierarchy. It is ultimately antipatriarchal in its claims.

The people agree to the covenant (v. 8), but the outcome remains to be seen. They have not yet grasped the full implications of God's claim, and of the transformation that must take place in them if they are truly to be God's people. The New Testament appropriates this idea of a "priestly people" for the church (cf. 1 Pet. 2:9). The church's task, also, is to mediate the knowledge of God to the world. Like Jeremiah, it is called to be faithful.

SECOND LESSON: ROMANS 12:1-8

The length of this reading varies widely among the lectionaries. The first two verses are the most clearly distinct unit, because they are the introductory heading to the whole section of exhortation that follows (chaps. 12–13). The breaks in the other readings are somewhat artificial, especially because the chapter is rather disorganized and there is little in the way of logical sequence to the various exhortations.

In light of all that has gone before, Paul makes an urgent appeal to the Christian women and men at Rome to commit themselves wholly ("present your bodies," i.e., the whole living, flesh-embodied person) to God's service. It is this total dedication of self, symbolically described as "a living sacrifice," that is the authentic worship befitting a transformed human life.

Two aspects of this passage have proved problematic: For one thing, the notion of sacrifice has been controversial for centuries between Protestants and Catholics. This reading provides a good occasion for reflecting on the genuine meaning of the notion of "sacrifice" in our modern religious understanding; it need no longer constitute a stumbling block to ecumenical dialogue. The "sacrifice" intended here is a free self-surrender to God, which in itself is the spiritual (rational, moral, or mystical) worship that is required. The process of renewed thinking enlightened by love is the same as is described in Phil. 1:9-10.

The second problem is more subtle. If not properly treated, this text can reinforce patterns of submission and domination. This is where sensitivity to the audience is highly important. Paul's exhortation is addressed to the *whole* Christian body. His demand is for a complete response, a surrender of the whole person to God. As a result of this renewal, all believers are enabled to discern God's will and to follow it. The process begins in God and returns to God. Nothing in the passage can or should be used to require the submission of some people to others. (See Beverly Roberts Gaventa, "Romans," *Women's Bible Commentary,* 319.)

Beginning with v. 3, Paul develops the idea of the gifts that are to be exercised within and on behalf of the community, the concrete content of the "living sacrifice." This passage is often compared to the similar listing in 1 Cor. 12:4-31, but there are significant differences. For one thing, the items listed here are not the "spiritual gifts," such as tongues, that were at issue in Corinth. In Romans, the gifts are not connected with the Spirit, nor is their diversity traced to the Spirit. In Corinth, Paul confronted a group of people who insisted that the infusion of the Spirit given them at baptism bestowed on them not just one, or some, but *all* spiritual gifts, and that the exercise of those gifts was governed by the Spirit alone. Paul countered by trying (without great success) to prescribe a division of gifts and a selective exercise of them. Here in Romans, he is addressing a group of churches with which he is not personally familiar, and his approach is a good deal more tentative. He uses the "body" metaphor, but the reference is to a moral union, just as one might speak of "the body politic." It is not a question of "the body of Christ," although the members are "one body *in* Christ." It is Christ who is the principle of union and mutual service.

The gifts in question are, except for prophecy, human talents that are to be used for the good of the whole. Prophecy is to be exercised "in proportion to faith" (v. 6, cf. v. 3); this seems to refer to the content rather than the quality of one's belief. In light of v. 3, Paul seems to be saying that the "measure of faith" is what proportions the distribution of gifts so that they will be adequate for the needs of the whole: not too much of any one, nor too little, but a "balanced diet" for the corporate body.

The other gifts are ministry (or service), teaching, exhortation, generous giving, leadership, and compassion. We may note that "leadership" was rendered in older translations as "giving aid." Similarly, the deacon Phoebe was formerly described as a "helper," though she is now called a "benefactor" (NRSV) and could with equal justice be described simply as a "leader" or "presider." (The Greek word for "leader" or "patron" in v. 8 is cognate with the title applied to Phoebe in 16:2. It is worth noting that translators and commentators have often hesitated to translate "leader," "apostle," "deacon," and the like, when the title clearly applies to a woman, although they have no difficulty with the terms applied to men or indeterminate persons assumed to be men.)

Verses 9-13 begin a sequence of traditional catechesis. The exhortations are standard, not only to Christian, but also to Jewish and Greek ethical exhortation. A community that expects to last will certainly apply itself to mutual love and honor; although these words would have been heard differently by people in a severely hierarchical social context, their egalitarian implications are certainly available for us today.

GOSPEL: MATTHEW 16:21-28

This pericope contains the "first passion prediction" as well as a series of sayings on discipleship. In Matthew, as in Mark, it represents an important turning point in the story, but Matthew, unlike Mark, separates this episode from Peter's confession by inserting the words, "from that time." These words occur only twice in Matthew's Gospel: at 4:17 when Jesus begins his preaching in Galilee, and here as he prepares to leave Galilee and go to Jerusalem to suffer. Verse 21 stands as a summary heading for the second part of the Gospel.

The second part of the reading, vv. 22-23, is a dialogue between Jesus and Peter. For Mark, it was essential not merely to confess Jesus as the Messiah, but to understand clearly what that title means, for Jesus and for believers. The disciples, led by Peter, do not understand and have to be brought up short. In Mark, Jesus' reply to Peter touches all the disciples. For Matthew, the issue is not understanding, but faith (the disciples do understand, as Peter's confession has shown). Peter, again the spokesperson as in the previous story, is still an *oligopistos*, a person with little faith. He has to be rebuked for his meager faith.

Mark does not report Peter's words to Jesus, but Matthew gives them in terms of a polite, even deprecating wish that could be translated, "May the merciful God spare you this fate." Still, Jesus turns sharply on him, calling him "Satan," and punning on Peter's designation as "the rock" by calling him a "stumbling block" or "stone of stumbling" (*skandalon;* cf. Isa. 8:14). When Peter's thinking came from God (16:17) he was "solid as a rock." Here, by contrast, where he is thinking in human terms, he is a stone to stub your toe on. Rockiness has its good and its bad sides!

Peter's attitude is much like that of Jeremiah; it is a vision of God's justice. It is simply not right that God's faithful prophet should suffer. Jesus is presented as thinking like the God who responds harshly to Jeremiah: God has different standards, and plans that human beings do not fathom. It is not for human beings to give orders or have second thoughts about God's plans. The only place for a disciple is the one assigned to Peter: *behind* the master as a follower.

While it is certainly probable that Jesus foresaw the possible tragic outcome of his life, it would be too much to expect that he would have predicted his death in these precise terms. The prediction has been formulated in light of Scripture and of the church's knowledge of the actual events. Jerusalem is where the prophets go to die. The "elders and chief priests and scribes" make up the ruling council, the Sanhedrin; it is noteworthy that no Pharisees, as such, are mentioned. "The third day" as the day of resurrection is a reference to Hos. 6:2. In saying that these things are "necessary," Jesus not only refers to fulfillment of Scripture, but to the apocalyptic notion of a series of unavoidable events presaging the end of the age, all part of a divine plan.

Confronted with the death of their leader, and thus with their own mortality, the disciples (and Matthew's community) try to avoid the issue. The evangelists, however, hammer home the reality with a series of sayings on the cost of discipleship. Matthew has two versions of the discipleship sayings; the other is found in 10:32-33, 38-39. He has Jesus address them solely to the disciples, and not to "the crowd," as in Mark. These are instructions for the Christian community, as was the Sermon on the Mount. The last two verses present an apocalyptic picture of the rewards of discipleship. Again there are special Matthean touches: The Son of Man comes as judge, not as advocate, and "his reign" is at the end of time. It is not the "coming of the reign in power" that Mark envisioned. The settling of accounts is already being removed from the earthly sphere, though it would be wrong to think that Matthew expected an indefinite delay of the Parousia. The language is that of the Old Testament (cf. Ps. 62:13; Prov. 24:12).

It is typical of Matthew to make the practical actions of life the measure by which we will be judged, but it is not a matter of counting up individual acts and weighing them in the scale. It is the whole tenor of one's life, one's praxis overall, that will count in the end. Through the whole process of losing, and thereby finding, life the Christian arrives at its ultimate fulfillment. The only judge of this "successful losing" will be the one who has endured it all before us and who returns as the glorious "Son of man" (or "human one") at the end, an end that Jesus, and later Matthew, expected in the very near future.

As with the reading from Paul, the preacher should be attuned to the audience in speaking of these injunctions to self-denial and "taking up the cross." Even a text with positive values can be used for bad ends, as when this particular passage is applied to encourage or even require a battered woman to remain with her abusive husband because the situation is her "cross"—no matter if it prove equally lethal. Just as the Jesus sayings do not treat the "cross" as something literal, but as an image of the worst sufferings a disciple may encounter, so the sayings cannot be applied literally and evenly to those whose "crosses" are of styrofoam and those whose burdens are of lead.

Sixteenth Sunday after Pentecost

Lutheran	Roman Catholic	Episcopal	Common Lectionary
Ezek. 33:7-9	Ezek. 33:7-9	Ezek. 33:7-11	Exod. 19:16-24
Rom. 13:1-10	Rom. 13:8-10	Rom. 12:9-21	Rom. 13:1-10
Matt. 18:15-20	Matt. 18:15-20	Matt. 18:15-20	Matt. 18:15-20

FIRST LESSON: EZEKIEL 33:7-9

This chapter of the book of Ezekiel concludes the admonitions to Jerusalem and describes the city's fall in vv. 21-22. That event is prefaced, in vv. 1-9, by a renewal of Ezekiel's call to be a prophetic sentinel or watcher. The overall theme of the chapter is God's desire for the people's repentance (cf. v. 11), even though it seems to be too late for most of them. YHWH is bringing the attack on the city, but YHWH has also chosen a watcher to warn the people.

The verses chosen for today's reading constitute a recommissioning of the prophet, following a description of the sentinel's task in terms of a parable in vv. 1-6. The words of vv. 7-9 are an almost verbatim repetition of Ezek. 3:17-19, and with much the same force: The prophet must issue a warning to the people or his own life is forfeit. However, in chapter 3 the instruction continues with the consequences of a warning given to the righteous. If righteous people have turned away from God and committed iniquity, they may die if not warned, and the consequences will fall on the prophet; however, if they are warned and respond to the warning, they may be saved. Nothing is said in either place about a conversion of the wicked.

Chapter 33 envisions a situation in which the people have fallen victims to despair: They say they are too sinful to live (v. 10). The prophet or watcher must insist that all who listen to the warning will save their lives. It is *not* too late for conversion (the expression "turn back" occurs three times in v. 11). As the previous passage repeated chapter 3, so this section reiterates chapter 18. The prophet's task is not finished when the city has perished. God still desires the people's repentance, and continued warnings must be issued to the survivors, so that they will not despair over their weakness and guilt.

There has been a tendency among exegetes to give an individualistic interpretation to this passage. For example, Walther Eichrodt says (*Ezekiel: A Commentary* [Philadelphia: Westminster, 1970], 447), "Thus the order given to the prophet, as we understand it, is to become one who gives warning to the individual wicked [person] or lapsed pious [person]." Ralph W. Klein (*Ezekiel*, 28–32) vigorously counters this approach, pointing out that the warning given is to "the house of Israel" (vv. 7, 10). The destruction of God's people, Israel, is at stake; individual sins are of such great importance because they are the cause of the impending destruction of God's holy community. God's will is that the sinners should repent and Israel be saved. So also in the Gospel reading for today, the focus should not be on individuals as such. The community has a responsibility to preserve itself from danger, but the emphasis lies on its making every effort in its power to restore lost members to full communion.

ALTERNATIVE FIRST LESSON: EXODUS 19:16-24

This account of the theophany at Sinai completes the narrative in chapter 19. It follows the story of the people's arrival and Moses' first ascent of the mountain as described in last Sunday's reading; the two are separated only by an account of the purification of the people preparatory to their encounter with God. The whole purpose of the theophany is that the people will acknowledge that God is really present and speaking to Moses. They are to understand that what Moses will say to them afterward (including the Ten Commandments) comes from God.

The mountain is sacred because God descends upon it. Once that has occurred, the whole mountain is charged, like an electrical field, with the divine presence. To enter that sphere is to become charged as well with the divine holiness, and consequently to become dangerous to others, like a high-voltage wire. Such a person must be removed from the community without being touched, that is, by stoning or shooting, so that the spark will not be transferred to others; this is the import of the warnings that the Lord may "break out upon them" so that "many of them [will] perish."

Another way of explaining the necessity of keeping the people at a distance is that "seeing God" is incompatible with human life as such. A full vision of God would put an end to human freedom, because God is irresistible. Only the mediators like Moses can see God "face to face," in order that they may perform their mediating function, but even in their case some ambiguity must remain. Ultimately, there can be only one mediator between God and humanity: the one who shares fully in the nature of each.

In vv. 16-24 we read of Moses' second ascent of the mountain. (Verse 25 completes the chapter with the note that Moses descended to tell the people what God had said.) Verses 16, 17, and 19 are from the Elohist source; the references are to "God" (= *ĕlōhîm*). Here God speaks in the thunder, that is, from the sky, as is appropriate to the name "Elohim." The remainder of the pericope is from the Yahwist source and speaks of "the LORD" (= YHWH); in these passages, the Lord speaks from the fire, just as the same Lord had spoken to Moses from the fiery bush in the previous Sinai theophany. The fire in the bush has been replaced by a much greater fire that covers the whole mountain.

The theophany is described in language appropriate to a storm ("thunder and lightning," "thick cloud"), like other theophanies in the Bible (e.g., Exod. 15:8, 10; Judg. 5:4-5; Pss. 18:7-15; 29:1-11; 77:16-20) and in ancient Ugaritic literature. The smoking mountain in v. 18 has suggested to some that there is a second description of the theophany in terms of a volcano, but this seems unlikely, because one cannot approach or ascend an active volcano and, historically speaking, there were no such mountains in the region at the time of the Exodus. In addition, comparable literature does not contain evidence of volcano theophanies.

The "smoke" and "trumpets," instead, appear to be elements of later liturgical reenactments of the Sinai events, which enabled people of subsequent generations to participate (one might even say "sacramentally") in the experience of Sinai. The "kiln" is more properly a fire pot used to symbolize the fire on the mountain— a mountain that, by this time, is Mount Zion, the successor to Sinai.

Verses 19-25 emphasize the great, even infinite, distance between YHWH and the people, and the vital mediating role of Moses. The people "hear" God and Moses speaking together (v. 19) while Moses is still in their midst. Only then (v. 20) does Moses go up the mountain to meet God alone. Once the covenant has been made, however, the whole people will become "holy," sacred to YHWH, and it will be possible for YHWH to dwell in their midst, first in the Tabernacle and then in the Temple.

SECOND LESSON: ROMANS 13:1-10

(For commentary on Rom. 12:9-21, see the previous Sunday.)

Romans 13:1-10 is a passage that has given modern commentators great difficulty, not only because of its content, but even more because of the history of its interpretation. It is of the utmost importance to read it in the context in which it occurs, and in terms of the actual situation within which it was written, and not to make of it a blanket instruction for Christians in their approach to governing authorities in all times and places.

Paul is addressing a group of Christians living in the capital of the empire, people who would be particularly close to the problem of authority. There is no evidence of persecution of Christians at Rome by this date, other than the expulsion of the Jews under Claudius occasioned, apparently, by quarrels between Christian and non-Christian Jews. However, Paul sees a danger that Christians, who regard themselves as citizens of another world, might question their continued allegiance to civil authority. He offers a solution in general terms more or less parallel to the attitude indicated by the response to the question of taxation in Matt. 22:16-21. His theme, stated in v. 1, is that God is the ultimate basis of all earthly authority, according to the principle in Prov. 8:15-16: "By me kings reign, and rulers decree what is just; by me rulers rule, and nobles, all who govern rightly." That rulers might not "govern rightly" does not enter Paul's consideration at this point. He simply takes it for granted that the imperial government is, on the whole, just, and therefore has the authority granted by God to rulers.

The order of themes in the text is: behavior within the Christian community (12:9-13); behavior within society (12:14-21)—including relations with enemies—and finally, the means by which the good (who are not to avenge themselves, cf. 12:19) are to be protected, namely the state authorities (13:1-7). Christians, like all other members of the empire, should obey the laws, pay taxes, and even respect the tax collectors, never a popular class in any society. The verb for "being subject" to the authorities (v. 1) derives from a word stem for "order." It is the word used throughout the New Testament for participation in the hierarchical "order of things" that the authors of these books (though not the whole tradition) regarded as divinely given. On the whole, Paul was a good deal more conservative in his respect for the social order as it existed than were some of his converts, notably free women and slaves of both sexes.

In Paul's time, religious movements tended either to divinize the highest authorities (as in the cult of the emperor) or to demonize them (as we see in the book of Revelation). The effect in either case was to heighten fear of rulers. The thrust of Paul's argument is to defuse that fear and awe, because those in authority are really only subjects carrying out the will of God, who is the true source of all authority. Surprisingly—to us, at least—Paul never mentions that the definition of good and evil behavior belongs to God alone. The delegated nature of authority is stressed three times: in vv. 1, 4, and 6. Believers ought to carry out their social obligations, trusting confidently that they are thereby fulfilling God's will.

In vv. 8-10, Paul sums up the whole of the Mosaic law in the new dispensation, and of his own ethical instruction in these chapters: "Love one another." This is the one debt (cf. v. 7) that is never fully paid, the single thing we continually owe to one another. The passage combines a list of commandments from the "second table" (obligations toward other people) in the order given in the Septuagint text of Deut. 5:17-21 with a sentence that echoes a saying of Jesus (cf. Mark 12:28-34): Love is the fulfilling of the law. In 12:8 Paul presented sisterly and brotherly love as the essence of the Christian life; in 12:14-21 he extended the obligation of love to enemies; now, in 13:8-10, he sums up the whole section by presenting love as the fulfillment of *all* obligations. "Neighbor" no longer means only fellow Jews or fellow Christians; in this context it is clear that Paul extends it to everyone. Paul has already said that Christ is the goal or "end" of the law (10:4); therefore love, the motive for Christ's whole existence and saving activity (8:34-35) can also be said to be the law's fulfillment. From that point on, love has become the measure of all Christian conduct. Properly applied, it achieves everything that the law stood for. Moreover, love and law are mutually supportive. Love is not something sentimental, something we are free to give or withhold. It is God's *law* that we love one another, because God has loved us and demonstrated that love in Jesus' cross and resurrection.

Clearly, this text cannot be preached "as is" in a world in which, quite obviously, the "legally constituted" governing authorities so often act unjustly, not to say barbarously, toward some or all of the people subject to them. A dialogue with Paul's perceptions—of hierarchy, of the sources of authority—is called for. The insights of liberation theology, of black theology, of feminist, womanist and *mujerista* exegesis and social criticism should be brought into play. According to them, the real locus of authority is the experience of oppressed people. Only they can offer the necessary critique to challenge the perspective of the "historical winners" projected in this text.

GOSPEL: MATTHEW 18:15-20

This section from the "community discourse" (Matt. 18:1-35) suggests a three-step procedure for the disciplining of recalcitrant community members. A brief admonition to correction of a brother or sister, derived from the sayings source (cf. Luke 17:3) has been expanded in Matthew to form this pericope. The discourse as a whole is ostensibly a response to a question by "the disciples," and in that sense can be seen as addressed to all church members. However, the injunction not to despise "one of these little ones," followed by the parable of the lost sheep (vv. 10-14) indicates that Matthew is really thinking of instructions for community leaders. "Little ones" is a favorite Matthean term for Christian believers.

What, then, is a Christian, especially one in a position of authority, to do if "another member of the church (a brother or sister) sins"? The words "against you" are probably a scribal insertion derived from v. 21, so what is at issue here is presumably not a personal quarrel or conflict between two individuals, but rather the kind of "sin" that would be damaging to the community as a whole. Because this section immediately follows the parable of the lost sheep, we have been alerted to the seriousness with which God regards the loss of even one person. The tension between the parable and the procedure for eventual dismissal described in vv. 21-28 suggests that community members must go "all out" to avoid schisms and to win back any members who go astray.

The first step is a private interview with the sinner. If persuasion prevails, "you have [re]gained that one." The word for "gained" is a technical rabbinic term for missionary conversion (cf. Lev. 19:17, 18). If this step fails, a second interview should take place in the presence of two or three witnesses, as provided by Deut. 19:15, which is cited here. It is not clear whether they are to witness to the sin, or to the dialogue about it. The third step, if the first two have failed, is to present the matter to "the church," that is, the local Christian community. (This is the second of two uses of the word *church* in Matthew, the only one of the Gospel writers to use the term. The first occurrence in 16:18 is clearly a reference to the *whole* body of believers. Here it just as clearly means a local congregation. It derives from the late first-century situation in which Christians identified themselves as "church" [*ekklesia*] as distinguished from the "synagogue" of their former fellow believers.) A failure to persuade at this stage leads to excommunication, a drastic step that (especially in light of the parable) can be taken only when the welfare of the entire community is at stake. The description of the outcast as being like "a Gentile and a toll collector" presupposes a community made up largely of Jewish-Christian believers. A process like this was unknown in mainstream Judaism of the first century, but there was an almost identical procedure in use at Qumran, and the practice in Christian communities may have been influenced by contacts with or recruits from that community.

In vv. 18-20, Matthew develops this idea of church discipline along a path from law to theology. In v. 18, the disciples are given the same power to bind and loose that was granted to Peter in 16:19. The next verse assures them, in technical legal terminology, that God will respond to their prayers, here described as "claims" to be ratified; the terms could be used for a lawsuit or an out-of-court settlement. The climax is the assurance that "where two or three are gathered in my name, I am there among them" (v. 20). This is undoubtedly a post-Easter saying spoken through the mouth of one of the community's prophets. It is closely related to the beginning of Matthew's Gospel (1:23, the quotation from Isa. 7:14, "God is with us") and the end (28:20, "I am with you always"). When Christians are gathered, for prayer, study, or (in the present context) decision making, they are assured of the abiding presence of the risen Christ. The verse compares Christ both with the Torah and with the divine presence, the Shekinah. Note the parallel passage in Midrash Aboth 3:2: "If two or three sit together and the words of the Law [are spoken] between them, the Shekinah rests between them." Matthew's Christians gather to study Torah as fulfilled by Jesus, an effective riposte to their rivals in the nearby synagogue.

The context in which this pericope is located shows that Matthew and his community are far more concerned about retrieving repentant sinners than about disciplining them. Although the community must be on guard against those whose actions could rob the community of its Christian character, the loss of any member represents a failure, and no repentant sinner can be refused forgiveness, no matter how many times he or she falls away. This is true because Jesus, the friend of "toll collectors and sinners" is always in their midst.

Seventeenth Sunday after Pentecost

Lutheran	Roman Catholic	Episcopal	Common Lectionary
Gen. 50:15-21	Sir. 27:30—28:7	Sir. 27:30—28:7	Exod. 20:1-20
Rom. 14:5-9	Rom. 14:7-9	Rom. 14:5-12	Rom. 14:5-12
Matt. 18:21-35	Matt. 18:21-35	Matt. 18:21-35	Matt. 18:21-35

FIRST LESSON: GENESIS 50:15-21; SIRACH 27:30—28:7

Both the Genesis and Sirach readings are related to the Gospel theme of forgiveness. The Genesis reading and the Gospel are narrower in focus: They deal with forgiving one's brother (or sister). In the Genesis text these are brothers in the flesh, while in the Gospel they are one's fellow Christians. The reading from Sirach, on the other hand, has to do with forgiving one's "neighbor," which would imply at least all Jews and, in Christian interpretation, everyone else.

A second thing the two readings have in common is that, generically, they are both taken from the wisdom literature. The Joseph novella is a wisdom story displaced into the Pentateuch. Joseph is a wise man and a model of good conduct. The reading comes near the end of the novella. Jacob has died, and the old patterns of behavior reappear: Joseph's brothers, fearful that he will treat them as they once treated him, stage one last act of deception. They pretend that their father, before dying, had asked Joseph to forgive them. For the first time in the whole story, they ask for Joseph's forgiveness, but they do so in such an underhanded way that it is no wonder Joseph bursts into tears. His ultimate response sums up the whole narrative, repeating substantially what he had said to them on their first encounter in Egypt, in 45:5-9. Their intentions toward him had been evil (and no doubt still would be, except that he holds all the power); nevertheless, it was all part of God's good plan, and the ultimate results have been good rather than evil, thanks to God. That God's wisdom always prevails in the end, even bringing good out of evil, is the primary lesson intended by the authors of the story. A second point is that Joseph, the wise man, is a model of forbearance and forgiveness. Of course, one might say that, given his wealth and position, he can afford to be magnanimous. Still, he could offer a hint to many powerful people today.

On a psychological plane, the story sheds some light on the Gospel parable. Because Joseph's brothers are so treacherous and mean spirited, they can never fully believe that Joseph is a better person than themselves. They cannot trust anyone, because they know themselves to be untrustworthy. Similarly, the slave in the Gospel illustrates by his behavior toward his fellow servant that he is a treacherous man. We learn from his actions that he has not really experienced his master's forgiveness. He does not believe he has been forgiven, since his own actions illustrate that, in his heart, he does not acknowledge the possibility of forgiveness. The vicious circle of pitiless violence perpetrated by people who have never experienced pity or compassion is an all-too-familiar phenomenon in our own day. Jesus' call is to break the chain of violence by relentless forgiveness.

The Sirach reading follows a precedent set in the early wisdom literature, although the motive for action is not entirely altruistic. Proverbs 25:21-22 had counseled feeding and clothing one's enemies, thereby "heaping coals of fire upon their heads," a passage quoted by Paul in last week's reading from Romans. Sirach stretches the matter a bit farther, and comes close to the lesson of the Gospel parable: If one expects to be forgiven by God, one should also forgive one's neighbor. Those who are in covenant with God are obligated to overlook faults just as God does.

ALTERNATIVE FIRST LESSON: EXODUS 20:1-20

This very familiar text is the Elohist version of the Ten Commandments, similar to but not quite identical with the Deuteronomist's version in Deut. 5:6-21. Like Matthew 18, it is ultimately a rule for community life. The commandments of the "second table," that is, the six dealing with human relationships, have their ultimate rationale in those of the "first table," which order Israel's relationship to its God.

YHWH, Israel's God, has absolute claim to Israel's allegiance, because it is YHWH who brought Israel out of Egypt. Having laid legitimate claim to this people, and made good the claim, YHWH now has an absolute right to them. They had been Pharaoh's subjects, and now they are YHWH's. Consequently, they must not divide their allegiance among gods; they can have but one. Nor can they pick and choose among YHWH's commands, because, all together, these constitute the rule for life according to YHWH's plan.

Images were the ordinary means of encounter between people and their gods, and it was common to find one or more statues of gods in sanctuaries. In Israel, however, the aniconic tradition (of making no image for the deity) goes back very far. No authenticated image of YHWH has ever been found, although there is a depiction of a couple found at one sanctuary that may represent YHWH and his Asherah or spouse. The conviction underlying Israel's aniconic tradition remains significant: No lifeless thing can capture the image of this God who is always in relationship. The only true "image" of God is that creature-in-relationship, the human.

YHWH is not so much "jealous" as "passionate"—passionately committed to Israel. YHWH will not forget to punish sins: Their consequences will haunt later generations, because the people, the nation, does not exist only in one generation. They live in solidarity with those who have gone before and with those who will come after; what affects one generation affects all. This is worthy of reflection in our own day, when serious questions are raised about the consequences for our children of our destruction of the environment and irresponsible waste of resources.

The sabbath was an institution unique to Israel. There is a prescription here for *how* to observe the sabbath (vv. 8-10), and a rationale for *why* the sabbath is to be kept (v. 11). Time is not our possession. Like everything else, it belongs to God the creator, who has a right to determine how it shall be used. There seems to be a curious lapse in v. 10, in the listing of those who are obliged to keep the sabbath: The wife is not mentioned. "You" throughout the Decalogue is the masculine singular: These words are addressed only to the male members of the community. In fact, as is clear from this verse, it addresses the heads of households (see v. 17 also). Although women in Israel were not held to all the obligations of the Law, they certainly were expected to participate in the sabbath observance; yet here sons and daughters, menservants and maidservants, even cattle and foreigners in the land are mentioned, but not a word about the mother of the family. She appears to be subsumed in her union with her husband.

In the next verse, the mother reappears, this time as the subject of honor, together with the father. This illustrates an important aspect of patriarchal society: Its benefits were not equally distributed along gender or status lines; age also played a part. A mother had at least some control of her children and, in her old age, was entitled to their respect and support. The commandment is addressed to adult children. Refusal to honor parents would be a blow to the social fabric; if it is neglected, the promise of "long life in the land" will be threatened. In fact, violation of any of the Ten Commandments would be a breach of the covenant and would threaten the integrity of the community that exists only in and because of that covenant.

The commandments regarding killing, adultery, theft, and false witness, as well as coveting (taking action to steal or defraud) need to be read by Christians in light of Jesus' interpretation. They apply not merely to a narrow range of actions, but to whatever disorders human relationships. Respect for the integrity of others is the heart of the matter.

The final verses match 19:20-25, again underscoring Moses' role as mediator. The people are afraid of contact with God that could sweep them out of their world into the divine sphere—that, in short, would kill them.

SECOND LESSON: ROMANS 14:5-12

In this passage, Paul is addressing differences of opinion and practice within the Christian community at Rome. He speaks in more general terms than in his

SEVENTEENTH SUNDAY AFTER PENTECOST

letter to the Corinthians, because he is not personally acquainted with many of the Roman Christians. It appears that there are disagreements about diet and the observance of the sabbath; these are worth Paul's attention because they are causes of dissension within the communities, leading some to disdain others.

Paul's call is not merely for tolerance, but for a vigorous effort at mutual understanding. The true reconciliation begins when we acknowledge that "whether we live or whether we die, we are the Lord's."

Being liberated *from* bondage to sin, death, and law, we are freed *for* service to God. This is the same point made by the introductory passage of the Decalogue in Exodus 20: We are not free simply for the sake of being free, but for the will of God, which is our salvation. It is our union in service to God that is the basis for life in Christian society, just as "owning the covenant" and being faithful to it—to God's plan for human life—is the basis for Jewish life. For Christians, this involves acknowledging that Jesus is *kyrios*, Lord, with universal dominion over the dead and over the living.

The Old Testament quotation in v. 11 is conflated from Isa. 49:18 and 45:23 in the Septuagint Greek version. The last part was also used in Phil. 2:10-11, where the sense is close to the original. Here the verb for "give praise," *exomologēstai*, has the sense of "admitting," or "confessing" one's deeds before God as judge. Fortuitously, the Pauline reading on this Sunday corresponds in part to the subject of the Gospel reading: Namely, that because Christians bend the knee and confess their sins before God, they should not presume to pass judgment on one another.

GOSPEL: MATTHEW 18:21-35

This story illustrates and reinforces the instructions that went before it. Matthew has taken a teaching of Jesus from the sayings source (cf. Luke 17:4) and converted it into a dialogue with Peter, who again appears as the spokesperson for the disciples. The parable really follows and explicates Matt. 6:12, 14, 15, the instruction in the Sermon on the Mount about forgiving.

When he suggests forgiving a brother or sister (that is, a fellow Christian) seven times, Peter thinks he is being extraordinarily generous, but Jesus' instruction to forgive seventy-seven (or seventy times seven) times goes unimaginably far beyond that. The great number effectively means: Forgive without any limit. This reverses the bloodthirsty boast of Lamech in Gen. 4:24: "If Cain is avenged sevenfold, truly Lamech seventy-sevenfold." This time it is a question of sins "against me," that is, personal affronts against fellow community members. The echo of the story of Cain reminds the hearers of the possible consequences of disputes between "brothers."

The dialogue is not quite appropriate to introduce the parable, where the issue is not the quantity of forgiveness (since there is no repetition), but its quality as imitative of God's forgiveness. The point of the parable, as Matthew has allegorized it, is effectively the same as in the reading from Sirach: Those whom God has forgiven are obligated to forgive others. The "slaves" are evidently high officials, not menials, and the amount of the first man's debt is absurdly great. He could have been a tax farmer, entitled to collect the king's revenues and keep a percentage for himself. To get some grasp on how much money "ten thousand talents" represented, we need only point out that the entire revenue of Herod's kingdom for a whole year was about nine hundred. If this man were the overseer of Herod's property, he would have to have absconded with the whole proceeds for more than ten years! (In other words, this is an exaggerated sum, the highest conceivable number. Its exorbitancy matches the seventy-sevenfold forgiveness prescribed in the introductory dialogue.) Clearly, such a debt could never be repaid; the sale of the family and property could serve as punishment but would never recover what is lost. The top price for a slave was only about one-fifth of a talent. In modern terms, it would be rather like asking one guilty individual to repay the entire losses of the savings and loan fraud of the 1980s. The king is extraordinarily generous in both forgiving the debt and even describing it, in the Greek of v. 27, as a "loan." In light of this, the slave's attitude toward his fellow slave, who owes him a sum equal to no more than one hundred days' wages for a laborer, is shocking beyond words. (This person owes one hundred denarii, or one one-hundredth of a talent. In other words, if the first servant owed $10,000, this servant's proportional debt would be one cent!) Here is a strongly cautionary message for those who earlier in the discourse (v. 18) had been given the power to "bind and loose." God's forgiveness is granted freely and without limit, and therefore love must temper even the exercise of power and discipline in the community.

In the story, the first debtor asks for tempered justice (more time), even though it is ludicrously impossible for him to repay his debt. What he receives, instead, is mercy. Without that part of the story, his proceeding in pressing his creditor to repay the one hundred denarii would be perceived simply as a just demand on his part. But in light of the king's generosity, the slave's failure to extend mercy in turn makes him *unjust* and even drives the king to an unjust act (rescinding his remission of the debt). In light of mercy, justice that is not tempered and even overruled by mercy is not even justice! Matthew draws the moral that those who put limits on their own forgiveness will (in the judgment, which Matthew has in mind, cf. v. 35) have limits placed on them by God.

We may look at these readings in a different light if we consider their implications for women members of the community. In both the Exodus passage (the Ten Commandments) and the Gospel, women are regarded as men's property, one thing among others to be coveted, stolen, or sold. While Jewish law did not under any circumstances allow for the sale of a wife (*m. Soṭa* 3.8), Greek and Roman laws were different, and it is by no means certain that such a thing was unknown in the Palestine of Jesus' time. Matthew's hearers would certainly have been aware that whole families could be sold into slavery because of debt or disaster. We are even more shocked at the idea, and yet the position of women in any patriarchal society is always precarious to a greater or lesser degree. For example, a current debate in a nearby city over whether retired female firefighters should be allowed to continue receiving their pensions if they marry (a question that never arises for male retirees) shows that the notion that a wife should be dependent on her husband is by no means dead. The fact is that such dependence puts her not only at his mercy but at the mercy of whatever misfortunes befall him. The wife in the story is the victim of her husband's crime, a circumstance that is all too often repeated today. True Christian equality requires that no one be the property of another, and that no one exist solely for the benefit of another, but that, as Paul says, "Whether we live or die, we are the Lord's." Not, as Milton had it, "He for God only; she for God in him," but all alike for the Lord.

Eighteenth Sunday after Pentecost

Lutheran	Roman Catholic	Episcopal	Common Lectionary
Isa. 55:6-9	Isa. 55:6-9	Jon. 3:10—4:11	Exod. 32:1-14
Phil. 1:1-5, 19-27	Phil. 1:20c-24, 27a	Phil. 1:21-27	Phil. 1:21-27
Matt. 20:1-16	Matt. 20:1-16	Matt. 20:1-16	Matt. 20:1-16

FIRST LESSON: ISAIAH 55:6-9

This chapter, with its summons to Mount Zion, marks the end of Second Isaiah. Verse 6 should read: "Seek the LORD *where* he may be found, call upon him *where* he is present." This is a summons to Israel to gather in the Lord's sanctuary. The conduct prescribed in verse 7 is that appropriate for people who are entering the divine presence. The wicked should abandon their ways, the unrighteous their wrong purposes, so that God may have mercy on them.

This passage in Isaiah parallels the tender words of Jer. 29:11-14: "For surely I know the plans I have for you, says the LORD, plans for your welfare and not for harm, to give you a future with hope. Then when you call upon me and come and pray to me, I will hear you. When you search for me, you will find me; if you seek me with all your heart, I will let you find me, says the LORD, and I will restore your fortunes and gather you from all the nations and all the places where I have driven you, says the LORD, and I will bring you back to the place from which I sent you into exile." After all their sufferings, Israel will return and find YHWH again in the Temple.

The "ways" of the wicked in v. 7 and the "ways" of Israel in v. 8 are not the same thing. In v. 8, the reference is to the people's doubt and lack of faith, their hesitation to trust YHWH's promises. The difference between God's saving plan for Israel and Israel's hesitation and self-doubt is as enormous as the distance between earth and heaven.

The emphasis on God's mercy combined with the statement that God's thoughts are not like human thoughts or God's ways like human ways occasions the use of the reading on this Sunday, in conjunction with the parable of the laborers in the vineyard, who are paid according to the owner's (i.e., God's) good pleasure, and not according to their own ideas of justice.

ALTERNATIVE FIRST LESSON: JONAH 3:10—4:11

This is another story of the differences between divine ideas of what is right and the judgment of human beings—in this case, one specific human being,

Jonah. The story takes up at the point where, having listened to Jonah's prophecy of destruction, the people of Nineveh have repented. As a result, God spares them. (Verse 10b repeats almost exactly God's response to Moses' prayer on behalf of Israel in Exod. 32:14. What Israel experienced in its early days, Nineveh experiences now.) This action in no way corresponds to what Jonah thinks should have happened. Jonah is angry, and Jonah sulks. He tells God, "I told you so!" and explains that this was the reason for his disobedience in the first place: He was afraid that, if warned, the Ninevites might repent, and he did not want to be the instrument of God's pardon to such despicable people as the Assyrians. His description of God's character, "gracious and merciful, slow to anger and abounding in steadfast love, ready to relent from punishing" echoes similar descriptions in Exod. 34:6-7; Num. 14:18; Neh. 9:17; Pss. 86:15; 103:8; 145:8-9. (The closest parallel is Joel 2:13, a promise to Jerusalem.) It recurs so frequently that it is almost a creedal formula, and it may well derive from a cultic context. In any case, Israel had for many centuries known that its God was gracious and merciful, even to sinners and reprobate foreigners.

Jonah, on the other hand, insists that God must conform to the ways of human justice; otherwise, God is capricious and life is ultimately absurd. The question is as modern as today: Why should anyone keep the law when the rewards for breaking the law are as good or better? Jonah allies himself with the prophet Malachi's opponents, who say: "It is vain to serve God . . . evildoers not only prosper, but when they put God to the test they escape" (Mal. 3:14-15). From Jonah's point of view, he is better off dead, because he has been party to an injustice. (Note the ironic contrast to 1 Kings 19:4, in which Elijah wishes himself dead because the people of Israel did *not* respond to his preaching.)

Jonah goes outside the city to pout; clearly he cannot bear to look at the happy faces of the Ninevites. Instead of examining himself, he waits for a change in the city. Perhaps it will relapse and be destroyed after all! God responds with an act of kindness toward the unhappy prophet, by making a castor oil plant grow and shade Jonah's hut. Jonah's joyful response contrasts sharply with his anger at God's kindness toward the people of the city. To teach him a lesson, God sends a worm to sap the plant's life, and then the searing sirocco from the desert to finish it off. Jonah is ready to die again. It seems a further proof of God's unfairness: First God showered the unworthy Ninevites with love; now the faithful prophet (as Jonah sees himself, despite all his recalcitrance) is deprived of even a little shade. God repeats the question God had posed to Jonah just before this episode: "Is it right for you to be angry?"

This puts Jonah on the horns of a dilemma: If he says "no," he will admit that God is sovereign and Jonah has no right to question God's doings. If he says "yes," he admits that God's having pity on Jonah is a good enough reason to spare a creature from destruction, and by extension this is also true of God's action toward the people and animals in Nineveh. Jonah chooses the second option, and God drives home the point. What Jonah had received was not something he had in any way deserved: He did not plant or tend the vine; it was a pure gift. God has the right to extend and take away gifts as God chooses.

Martin Luther drew the parallel between this story and that of the workers in the vineyard, and other commentators have taken up his suggestion; hence its choice for the Episcopal lectionary for today. (For a detailed discussion and comparison, see Hans Walter Wolff, *Obadiah and Jonah: A Commentary*, translated by Margaret Kohl [Minneapolis: Augsburg, 1986], 155-77.)

ALTERNATIVE FIRST LESSON: EXODUS 32:1-14

In the continuing reading from Exodus, we now arrive at Israel's apostasy from the covenant they had just concluded with YHWH. Moses ascends the mountain for forty days and forty nights, during which he receives instructions for the building of the sanctuary in which YHWH will continue to dwell among the people. But the people are not satisfied with this timetable, nor with the proposed mode of YHWH's presence. They are anxious to get on the move, they need a God to accompany them, and they want a God who is visible and tangible, at least in representative form, like the gods of other nations. They take matters into their own hands.

In contrast to his importance elsewhere in the narrative, Aaron here appears in a bad light. He very quickly caves in to the people's demands and prepares a pair of golden statues of young bulls—a common form for divine figures in the Ancient Near East, or sometimes the throne figures on which the divine being rested. There is a deliberate and ironic parallel to the instructions for the ark that YHWH is in the process of giving to Moses. Once the figures are finished, a feast is held. Eating and drinking represented a sharing in the god's hospitality, and thereby becoming his or her client.

The whole story is modeled on historical events. According to 1 Kings 12:28-33, King Jeroboam led the people of the northern kingdom into apostasy by making two golden bulls and saying the very words that are attributed to Aaron in this story: "Here are your gods, O Israel, who brought you up out of the land of Egypt." (There are two statues, one for the sanctuary at Dan and the other for that at Bethel. Hence the plural, "gods.") The Elohist author is here projecting Jeroboam's apostasy into the original history of Israel; in other words, what we see here is "a typical Israel engaged in a typical sin" (see Michael Guinan, *The Pentateuch*, 67). The creation imagery even permits us to call it an "original sin." A conflict over modes and symbols of worship has been made to typify Israel's apostasy from its God. Politically, the story attacks both the monarchy and the Aaronide priesthood.

A dialogue between Moses and YHWH follows. When the people start misbehaving, they are suddenly Moses' people, and not YHWH's: "*Your* people, whom *you* brought up out of the land of Egypt, have acted perversely." This mimics what the people have been saying in vv. 1 and 4, but it also sounds like a domestic dialogue when one of the teenagers misbehaves: "Let me tell you what *your* son/daughter did today!" By saying, "Let me alone," God concedes Moses some say in the matter, and so provides a loophole for Moses to launch a counterargument. Moses turns the rhetoric around: "O Lord, why does your wrath burn hot against *your* people whom *you* brought out of the land of Egypt with great power and with a mighty hand?"

Moses has two significant arguments to make against YHWH's destroying the people. In domestic terms, they are "What will the neighbors think?" and "But you promised!" (Guinan, *The Pentateuch*, 67–68). YHWH is called upon to remember the promises given to the ancestors, and also to think of what the Egyptians will say—"I told you it was all a trick! Their god just wanted to destroy them!" In an honor-shame culture, these arguments hit hard. Fidelity to one's word in such a culture is sacred, and if YHWH goes back on the word once given, the result will be shame. One major theme in all this has been that, by rescuing Israel from Egypt, YHWH will gain glory and honor at the expense of the Egyptians. Logically, if YHWH destroys the people, the opposite will happen: YHWH will be shamed, and the Egyptians will gain vicarious honor at YHWH's expense. The argument is effective; YHWH relents.

SECOND LESSON: PHILIPPIANS 1:1-5, 19-27

The reading for today in the Lutheran lectionary includes the greeting at the beginning of the letter, while the other three lectionaries concentrate on the latter part of the chapter. The introductory verses contain the standard opening to a Hellenistic letter, expanded by some elements that are peculiar to Paul or special to this letter. One of the latter is the slave-master metaphor, which dominates the rhetoric of Philippians. Paul is a slave; Christ took the form of a slave, therefore the Philippians should serve one another.

Philippians is unique among the authentic Pauline letters in its mention of *episkopoi* as well as the *diakonoi* we meet elsewhere, for example, in Rom. 16:1. *Episkopoi* is frequently translated "bishops," but that conveys a church office that certainly did not exist, as such, in Paul's time. The word was common in Greek usage, and meant something like "overseer," especially the person in charge of financial affairs. The *episkopos* was something like the CFO, on a small scale. The greeting to *episkopoi* and *diakonoi* may reflect a greater degree of formal organization in the Philippian congregations than we find elsewhere at this date, or it may be related to the legal and commercial metaphor that pervades the first chapter.

Paul writes to the Philippians from prison, and it was long supposed that he was already in prison at Rome. This now seems less likely, especially because Paul evidently hopes to be released soon, and because he clearly has easy communication with Philippi, which would not be the case if he were far away in

Rome. More probably this imprisonment took place during Paul's relatively long residence at Ephesus.

The commercial metaphor in chapter 1 is that of a business partnership: The Philippians have entered a partnership with Paul for the spread of the gospel (v. 5). We learn in 4:15 that no other church has joined with him in such an arrangement. Such a partnership was undertaken by two or more individuals or groups for a particular purpose, and the death of one partner ended the arrangement. It could also be dissolved if the partners had a serious disagreement. Paul's repeated insistence that the Philippians should "be of one mind" (1:27; 2:2; 4:2) suggests that there may have been disagreements threatening the continued partnership. (We should note that "be of one mind" or "be of the same mind" could refer to disagreements between the Philippians—or some of them—on the one hand and Paul on the other hand, not merely to quarrels between members of the Philippian church. Therefore it is wrong simply to dismiss Euodia and Syntyche in 4:2 as two women whose quarreling between themselves has disrupted the church's life. They may just as well be, jointly, opposing Paul on some point.)

If Paul thinks there is a serious possibility of his being executed, the partnership is threatened in a different way. It may be dissolved by his death, or the rivalry that seems to exist within the community might lead to the breakup of the gospel enterprise. Paul urges that, no matter what happens, the Philippians should remain united. Although he speculates on its being "far better" for him to die and be with Christ, this is anything but a general doctrine of flight from the world, for he encourages the Philippians (v. 27) to "discharge your duty as citizens" (rather than "live your life," as in NRSV) in a manner worthy of the gospel. Philippi was a Roman *colonia,* with Roman law and Roman privileges of citizenship. Paul desires that the Christians there should be good citizens and good partners, all of which will benefit the gospel.

There were strong traditions of women's leadership at Philippi (according to the traditions in Acts, the first convert there was Lydia [Acts 16:14], and the letter mentions Euodia and Syntyche by name as those who have "struggled beside [Paul] in the work of the Gospel"). In spite of this, the letter is strongly oriented to the men of the community, not only by its commercial language (which at least some women, like Lydia, would well have understood) but even more by the pervasive athletic and military metaphors and by the insistence on the exercise of the duties of citizenship, for the political sphere was virtually closed to women. All of this excludes from consideration, to an even greater degree, those members of the community who were slaves, as will be seen in the discussion of next week's reading (the Christ hymn in Philippians 2). For the outcasts of society Paul's rhetoric was ambiguous at best.

GOSPEL: MATTHEW 20:1-16

The well-known parable of the workers in the vineyard is framed, in 19:30 and 20:16, by the dominical saying, "The first will be last, and the last will be first." The form is chiastic, because the order is reversed in 20:16 to "The last will be first, and the first will be last." This is a careful Matthean composition in which the parable is supposed to illustrate and furnish a midrash on the saying.

There is, however, not much in the parable itself that matches the saying, except for the reverse order in which the workers are paid. Its point is more like "Last and first will be equal." There is some clearly metaphorical language: Israel as God's vineyard was a familiar Old Testament topos (cf. Isa. 5:1-7); the last judgment as harvest is also familiar in Christian thought. Nevertheless, great care should be taken not to allegorize the parable. The householder clearly represents God, but beyond that we should be cautious in identifying the other characters (e.g., Christ as the steward).

The issue is one of justice versus compassion. The question the householder poses to the grumbling workers is essentially the same as the one God asks of Jonah: "Am I not allowed to do what I choose with what belongs to me? Or are you envious because I am generous?" (v. 15; this is probably a deliberate addition by Matthew). The answer is not as easy as it sounds. Is it unjust to give the same compensation to people who have only worked an hour as to those who have worked hard all day? Should not some receive more, others less? The denarius was the standard day's wage for a laborer, and would buy enough bread to sustain a small family for one day. Anything less was below subsistence, so a further issue arises: Is it just to pay a wage that is less than subsistence, whatever the circumstances?

It has been suggested that a better title for this parable would be "The Good Employer," or even "The Affirmative Action Employer." The latter title brings out the "sting" that it has even today. Those who oppose affirmative action are driven by a feeling that, somehow, they themselves are being cheated if other people "get something for nothing" or receive "unfair advantages," no matter what advantages they themselves have unconsciously enjoyed, they and those like them for generations past. The conviction is strong in all hearts that we have a right to what we have "earned." The idea behind this parable, that whatever we receive is essentially gift, meets with strong resistance. It comes very close, after all, to Marx's dictum: "From each according to ability, to each according to need." What an uncomfortable business it would be to be forced to admit that Karl Marx understood the gospel message better than we!

We can find this parable played out every day in America, on the streetcorners of our great cities. In Los Angeles, unemployed men, many of them recent immigrants, gather in the parking lot of a convenience store to wait for day labor. A few are chosen to work unloading a moving van, a few more for yard work, several for painting. Others stand all day, waiting and hoping. Their work is paid by the hour. Those hired early, even though they must work all day, are the lucky ones. They can feel confident that, at the end of the day (if they are not cheated by their employers), they will have enough money to sustain themselves and their families for another twenty-four hours, at least. The others wait with gnawing stomachs and anxious hearts. How much better to be working than to suffer the fear of want! And how unfair it would be of the lucky ones to begrudge the less fortunate a living wage to compensate for their fear and anxiety!

The parable, as we have it, defends Jesus' special concern for the marginal in society. They will easily identify with the last hired who rejoice in the householder's generosity. The problem will be to persuade the fortunate, the "good citizens," not to identify with the "hard working" all-day laborers, but to comprehend that nothing we have is earned. Everything, even life itself, is the gift of a generous God.

Nineteenth Sunday after Pentecost

Lutheran	Roman Catholic	Episcopal	Common Lectionary
Ezek. 18:1-4, 25-32	Ezek. 18:25-28	Ezek. 18:1-4, 25-32	Exod. 33:12-23
Phil. 2:1-5	Phil. 2:1-11	Phil. 2:1-13	Phil. 2:1-13
Matt. 21:28-32	Matt. 21:28-32	Matt. 21:28-32	Matt. 21:28-32

FIRST LESSON: EZEKIEL 18:1-4, 25-32

Today's readings are somewhat loosely focused around the theme of responsibility. The notion of individual responsibility is an important feature in the thought of the prophet Ezekiel. He came from a priestly family and reflects that background, in contrast to Jeremiah and the traditions with which he is associated. A Deuteronomistic oracle in the book of Jeremiah also quotes the proverb (Jer. 31:29) about the sins of ancestors falling on the younger generations, but in a very different sense. For that writer, the abrogation of this saying will be a feature of the restored Israel of the new covenant. This agrees with the deuteronomistic viewpoint of the books of Kings that the wicked deeds of generations of people in Israel and Judah resulted in the exile of a later generation. For them, the proverb held true. According to the oracle in Jeremiah, it is *"in those days,"* that is, in the days when God restores Israel, that "they shall no longer say: 'The parents have eaten sour grapes, and the children's teeth are set on edge.' "

For Ezekiel, on the other hand, the exiled generation is not entitled to blame their situation on those who went before them. It is their own fault that they are suffering, because they are at least as sinful as their ancestors, and their ancestors' deeds are irrelevant to their situation. As far as Israel's own legal practice is concerned, the principle is enunciated in Deut. 24:16: "Parents shall not be put to death for their children, nor shall children be put to death for their parents; only for their own crimes may persons be put to death." Ezekiel does not expect God's legal practice to be less just than that of Israel; therefore no one may suffer for another's crime.

In vv. 21-29, Ezekiel addresses a second question: Does bad behavior in the past limit one's chances for repentance? The positive principles are set out in vv. 21-24, and are similar to those in the parable of the watcher (see commentary for the Sixteenth Sunday after Pentecost). The following paragraph (vv. 25-29) begins and ends with the question of YHWH's being "unfair," in our translations. More probably, the word is not "unfair," but "unfathomable." The question is, Whose ways are more inscrutable, YHWH's or Israel's? Given a choice between

67

sinking down into death or repenting and receiving life, how can the people possibly choose the former? They cannot claim that they are the victims of their ancestors' wrongdoing, nor that their own sins are unforgivable. If anyone is a brick short of a load in this situation, it is not YHWH! The conclusion follows in vv. 30-32: YHWH's repeated call for the people's repentance, and renewed assurance (when will they ever believe it?) that YHWH does not desire their death, but rather life.

Ezekiel's emphasis on personal appropriation of the Torah, even when the people are no longer in the Land to which that divine plan belongs, and even when there is no longer any coherent community of Israel to which the plan can apply, is at variance with the attitude of the Pentateuch sources, especially the Deuteronomist(s). For those thinkers, God's plan was for Israel as a community in a particular place; existence outside the community was simply not envisioned. It was not individuals whom God sent into exile, nor was it individuals whom God restored to their Land. It was Israel, God's beloved child. Even Ezekiel addresses himself to a whole generation, not to individuals. As Ralph Klein has written, "What chapter 18 insists upon . . . is really not individualism, but the moral independence of the house of Israel. They are not limited by the deeds of previous generations or even by the sinful past of their own generation" (*Ezekiel*, 108). Jesus' own thinking was similar, for he saw his mission as the restoration of Israel, the community of God's own people. Consequently, we should resist any tendency that may appear to be implied in the readings to disassociate human behavior from its community context.

ALTERNATIVE FIRST LESSON: EXODUS 33:12-23

This reading from the book of Exodus, true to its location in the Pentateuch, reflects the idea of community solidarity and divine freedom to deal with Israel's (collective) sin and guilt. As before, Moses appears as the mediator who pleads on behalf of the guilty people.

After the people's breaking of the covenant by setting up the golden bulls, and the immediate punishment that resulted, a renewed covenant has to be given and accepted. However, YHWH tells Moses that, as a consequence of the people's breach of faith, YHWH will no longer accompany the people on their march. Instead, an angel will be sent as YHWH's representative. Moses is not satisfied with that, and enters into negotiations. There is nothing shy or self-deprecating about his attitude. He begins and ends with imperatives: "See!" "Consider!" Moses is uneasy about dealing with some strange "angel." Who might that be, and what about all the fine things YHWH has said in the past about knowing Moses by name? He reminds God once again that Israel is "*your* people." How will Moses know, how will the people know, and in particular, how will potential enemies know that Israel has been singled out as YHWH's people, if YHWH does not go with them? Once again God relents.

NINETEENTH SUNDAY AFTER PENTECOST

Moses is not fully satisfied. Apparently as a sign and seal to YHWH's agreement, Moses asks to see YHWH's glory. There is an affirmation of the magnitude of that glory in the statement that Moses cannot see YHWH's "face," but only the "back." There is also an assertion of God's freedom in v. 19: "I will be gracious to whom I will be gracious, and will show mercy on whom I will show mercy." This seems to be an echo of God's very name, "I will be who I will be." God's actions are the expression of who God is. Moses is, in fact, asking to see God's very self, as an assurance that God will fully dwell among the people. But God's true comfort is in the assertion of God's character, *who* God is: good and gracious, merciful as well as just.

SECOND LESSON: PHILIPPIANS 2:1-13

In this continuation of the reading from Philippians, we find Paul still speaking in terms of a partnership for the spread of the gospel, but going beyond the legal stipulations of partnership to prescribe a Christian mutuality in love. The phrases in v. 1 describe the characteristics of life "in Christ," which in Paul's theology sums up the essential of what it means to be Christian. The repeated insistence, in v. 2, on being "of the same mind, . . . being in full accord and of one mind" suggests that unanimity is a preoccupation of the apostle. There was probably one faction of the Philippian church that practiced such unanimity—that is, by sharing Paul's ideas—and one or more others that did not. The loving tone of the letter indicates that Paul believed he could win over his opponents more easily by words of kindness and persuasion than by threats or coercion. The reiteration of "be of one mind" prepares the addressees for the climax: "Let the same mind be in you that was in Christ Jesus" (v. 5).

In treating this passage, especially the magnificent Christ hymn in vv. 6-11, we must be careful to distinguish the situations of its first audience. Paul begins from a fairly good "place." He was a man, a Jew (thus member of a group respected in the ancient world for their monotheism and high ethical standards), and he had some learning. Many members of the communities he missionized would have shared those characteristics, or been of even higher status than he. On the other hand, there were others, perhaps a majority, who started from a very different rung on the social ladder. They were women, and/or Gentiles (perhaps not even Greeks, but foreigners of some type), and/or slaves, and/or illiterate. Clearly, a call to imitate Christ by "emptying oneself" of all one has brings with it very different implications for the "haves" than for the "have-nots."

The exhortations in vv. 3-4 to avoid "selfish ambition or conceit," but to "regard others as better than yourselves" and to "look . . . to the interests of others" already have an ominous ring from the have-not perspective. To those "above," they are a call to magnanimous condescension. To those "below," however, they are an admonition to keep their place, to remember who their "betters" are, and not to seek to rise above themselves.

The exhortation to be like Christ in becoming powerless, even taking the status of a slave, then, addresses itself to the powerful. Before they can preach the gospel, they must "empty themselves," as Paul frequently asserts that he has done. It is, to say the least, pointless to use this text as a weapon with which to strike down the ambitions of the powerless to rise above their abject condition, and yet the passage has been used in this way for centuries, particularly against women and slaves. The text as it stands is a potential scandal for a slaveholding society, indeed for any society in which social inequalities exist (see Sheila Briggs, "Can an Enslaved God Liberate? Hermeneutical Reflections on Philippians 2:6-11," *Semeia* 47 (1989): 135–53). To say that Christ Jesus was "in the form of God" and voluntarily became so poor as to take "the form of a slave" (that is, not just economically poor, but socially degraded) is shocking, to say the least, but the process does not end there. In raising up Christ Jesus, God has exalted all those who identify with him. They are no longer condemned to slavery and oppression, because of Christ's victory.

To defuse this text's power by making it either an affirmation of the status quo here or a promotion of "pie in the sky" consolation for the oppressed is not legitimate. If the text is an appeal for an attitude of service, as commentators usually assert, it is also (as they usually fail to say) a call for reversal of fortunes, not in the vague future, but already *now*, in light of what *has* happened in Christ. In this sense the text is ontological (about what *is*) rather than ethical (about how people ought to behave). In the wake of cross and resurrection there are no further distinctions in society, for all are to bow down to Jesus and confess him alone as Lord. That is God's dispensation and God's plan. Social arrangements to the contrary are out of joint.

GOSPEL: MATTHEW 21:28-32

Following the cleansing of the Temple and Jesus' dialogue with the chief priests and elders about authority, Matthew inserts three parables (the two children, the wicked tenants, and the marriage feast) to drive home the point that the Jewish authorities are acting wrongly. The parables contrast two kinds of Jews: the faithless leaders and the faithful outcasts, the latter represented by the tax collectors and prostitutes. The reference in v. 32 to John the Baptizer ties this story back to the preceding dialogue, in which Jesus had stumped the chief priests and elders by asking them about the authority behind John's baptism.

The state of the Greek text is confused. The RSV and NRSV, following the published text currently in use, have the first child refusing, then repenting and going into the vineyard, while the second assents and then does not go. The Roman Catholic lectionary, following some of the best Greek manuscripts, reverses the order: The first child answers, "aye aye, sir" but does not go; the second grumbles and then goes. This arrangement seems to match the Matthean context better. Since this parable and the two that follow it are all aimed at the Jewish authorities, it seems more logical that Jesus would show the "first" of God's children accepting the covenant but failing to carry it out (cf. Isa. 5:1-7 for Israel as God's vineyard). The younger child, then, the restored Israel represented by the repentant outcasts, having first resisted the covenant eventually does God's will. (Or this reversal may have occurred in the manuscript tradition precisely *because* it seems so logical, especially when the parable was wrongly interpreted, in the early centuries, in terms of Jews and Gentiles.)

A note on language: The Greek text of the parable is deliberately ambiguous about the gender of the persons involved. The one who has the two children is *anthropos,* a (genderless) human being; the younger pair are not *huioi,* "sons," but *tekna,* "children." In the situation given and the society depicted, of course these would normally be a father and two sons, as the English translation has it, but the ambiguity of the Greek allowed then and allows now for *all* to identify with the characters in the story. It is not simply a story about men.

As so often in the Gospel dialogues, Jesus forces his interlocutors to convict themselves out of their own mouths. "Which of the two did the will of the father?" Their answer will identify them as disobedient (see Luke's effective use of this device in the story of the good Samaritan). There is bitter irony in Jesus' response. Tax collectors and prostitutes are going into the reign of God ahead of the righteous. These are, be it noted, two groups of outcast *Jews;* this parable is not about Jew versus Gentile. The tax collectors were hated collaborators with the occupying Romans, often brutal and greedy as well; prostitutes consorted with and entertained the Roman troops and officials, and they were officially "sinners" by their very occupation. That Jesus, during his historical lifetime, actually associated with such people on a regular basis is a fixed element in the tradition (cf. Mark 2:15-17 and parallels). These people, the official outcasts, are those who are able to see and believe; by contrast, the "wise" in the society, the educated elite, are blind; even after they saw John preaching "the way of righteousness" (a favorite theme in wisdom literature and also at Qumran) they did not see, repent, or believe.

Still, we must insist that the people addressed here are not simply individuals who have, singly, a responsibility to repent and believe the good news. The call is to Israel, and the unlikely people who respond are the basis for the restored and renewed Israel. In Matthew's context, the call is to the church. The appeal is urgent: to the "refuseniks" to change their minds; to the "yea-sayers" to hold fast and not fail. The invitation is open to the leaders to be like the first (or second) child and join the successors of the tax collectors and prostitutes in the Christian community. The warning to the latter is also there: not to say "Lord" without doing God's will (cf. 7:21).

The finest commentary on this pericope is Flannery O'Connor's short story, "Revelation." Throughout the story, Mrs. Turpin enjoys her superiority to several "lower" social groups until, at the end, she sees a vision of all those "trashy" people going up to heaven, "shouting and clapping and leaping like frogs." Behind them, at the end of the procession, are the "respectable" people like herself and her husband who "had always had a little of everything and the God-given wit to use it right." These move forward "with great dignity, accountable as they had always been for good order and common sense and respectable behavior. They alone were on key. Yet she could see by their shocked and altered faces that even their virtues were being burned away . . ." (Flannery O'Connor, *The Complete Stories* [New York: Farrar, Strauss & Giroux, 1971], 508).